Juvenile Crime

Crime

OPPOSING VIEWPOINTS®

Other Books of Related Interest

Opposing Viewpoints Series

American Values
America's Children
America's Future
America's Prisons
America's Victims
Chemical Dependency
Child Abuse
Crime and Criminals
Criminal Justice
The Death Penalty
Drug Abuse
Education in America
The Family in America

Gangs
The Homeless
Illegal Immigration
Interracial America
The Legal System
Pornography
Poverty
Race Relations
Social Justice
Teenage Sexuality
Violence
War on Drugs
Welfare

Current Controversies Series

Alcoholism
Drug Trafficking
Family Violence
Gun Control
Hate Crimes
Illegal Immigration
Police Brutality
Teen Addiction
Violence Against Women
Violence in the Media
Youth Violence

At Issue Series

Domestic Violence
The Jury System
Legalizing Drugs
Rape on Campus
Single-Parent Families

Juvenile
Crime
OPPOSING VIEWPOINTS®

David Bender & Bruno Leone, *Series Editors*

A.E. Sadler, *Book Editor*
Scott Barbour, *Assistant Editor*

OPPOSING
VIEWPOINTS®
SERIES

Greenhaven Press, Inc., San Diego, CA

No part of this book may be reproduced or used in any form or by any means, electrical, mechanical, or otherwise, including, but not limited to, photocopy, recording, or any information storage and retrieval system, without prior written permission from the publisher.

Photo credit: Craig McClain

Greenhaven Press, Inc.
PO Box 289009
San Diego, CA 92198-9009

Library of Congress Cataloging-in-Publication Data

Juvenile crime : opposing viewpoints / A.E. Sadler, book editor;
    Scott Barbour, assistant editor.
        p.   cm. — (Opposing viewpoints series)
    Includes bibliographical references and index.
    ISBN 1-56510-516-8 (lib. bdg. : alk. paper). —
ISBN 1-56510-515-X (pbk. : alk. paper)
    1. Juvenile delinquency—United States. 2. Juvenile
delinquency—United States—Prevention. I. Sadler, A.E.
II. Barbour, Scott, 1963–   . III. Series: Opposing viewpoints
series (Unnumbered)
HV9104.J833   1997
364.3'6'0973—dc20   96-21961
                                                                     CIP

Every effort has been made to trace the owners of copyrighted material.

"Congress shall make no law . . . abridging the freedom of speech, or of the press."

First Amendment to the U.S. Constitution

The basic foundation of our democracy is the First Amendment guarantee of freedom of expression. The Opposing Viewpoints Series is dedicated to the concept of this basic freedom and the idea that it is more important to practice it than to enshrine it.

Contents

Chapter 3: What Factors Contribute to Gang-Related Juvenile Crime?

Chapter 4: How Can Juvenile Crime Be Combated?

Why Consider Opposing Viewpoints?

"The only way in which a human being can make some approach to knowing the whole of a subject is by hearing what can be said about it by persons of every variety of opinion and studying all modes in which it can be looked at by every character of mind. No wise man ever acquired his wisdom in any mode but this."

John Stuart Mill

In our media-intensive culture it is not difficult to find differing opinions. Thousands of newspapers and magazines and dozens of radio and television talk shows resound with differing points of view. The difficulty lies in deciding which opinion to agree with and which "experts" seem the most credible. The more inundated we become with differing opinions and claims, the more essential it is to hone critical reading and thinking skills to evaluate these ideas. Opposing Viewpoints books address this problem directly by presenting stimulating debates that can be used to enhance and teach these skills. The varied opinions contained in each book examine many different aspects of a single issue. While examining these conveniently edited opposing views, readers can develop critical thinking skills such as the ability to compare and contrast authors' credibility, facts, argumentation styles, use of persuasive techniques, and other stylistic tools. In short, the Opposing Viewpoints Series is an ideal way to attain the higher-level thinking and reading skills so essential in a culture of diverse and contradictory opinions.

9

In addition to providing a tool for critical thinking, Opposing Viewpoints books challenge readers to question their own strongly held opinions and assumptions. Most people form their opinions on the basis of upbringing, peer pressure, and personal, cultural, or professional bias. By reading carefully balanced opposing views, readers must directly confront new ideas as well as the opinions of those with whom they disagree. This is not to simplistically argue that everyone who reads opposing views will—or should—change his or her opinion. Instead, the series enhances readers' depth of understanding of their own views by encouraging confrontation with opposing ideas. Careful examination of others' views can lead to the readers' understanding of the logical inconsistencies in their own opinions, perspective on why they hold an opinion, and the consideration of the possibility that their opinion requires further evaluation.

Evaluating Other Opinions

To ensure that this type of examination occurs, Opposing Viewpoints books present all types of opinions. Prominent spokespeople on different sides of each issue as well as well-known professionals from many disciplines challenge the reader. An additional goal of the series is to provide a forum for other, less known, or even unpopular viewpoints. The opinion of an ordinary person who has had to make the decision to cut off life support from a terminally ill relative, for example, may be just as valuable and provide just as much insight as a medical ethicist's professional opinion. The editors have two additional purposes in including these less known views. One, the editors encourage readers to respect others' opinions—even when not enhanced by professional credibility. It is only by reading or listening to and objectively evaluating others' ideas that one can determine whether they are worthy of consideration. Two, the inclusion of such viewpoints encourages the important critical thinking skill of objectively evaluating an author's credentials and bias. This evaluation will illuminate an author's reasons for taking a particular stance on an issue and will aid in readers' evaluation of the author's ideas.

As series editors of the Opposing Viewpoints Series, it is our hope that these books will give readers a deeper understanding of the issues debated and an appreciation of the complexity of even seemingly simple issues when good and honest people disagree. This awareness is particularly important in a democratic society such as ours in which people enter into public debate to determine the common good. Those with whom one disagrees should not be regarded as enemies but rather as people whose views deserve careful examination and may shed light on one's own.

Thomas Jefferson once said that "difference of opinion leads to inquiry, and inquiry to truth." Jefferson, a broadly educated man, argued that "if a nation expects to be ignorant and free . . . it expects what never was and never will be." As individuals and as a nation, it is imperative that we consider the opinions of others and examine them with skill and discernment. The Opposing Viewpoints Series is intended to help readers achieve this goal.

David L. Bender & Bruno Leone,
Series Editors

11

Introduction

On the evening of January 21, 1995, in San Diego, California, fourteen-year-old Tony Hicks shot and killed Tariq Khamisa, a twenty-year-old pizza deliveryman, while attempting to rob him of pizza and cash. Subsequently, under a new law that lowered to fourteen the age at which an accused killer can be tried as an adult, Hicks became the youngest person ever to be tried and convicted for murder in California. At his sentencing in June 1996, Hicks said to the judge, "I still don't know why I shot Tariq. I didn't really want to hurt him. I'm sorry." Despite this expression of remorse, Hicks was sentenced to twenty-five years to life in prison. He will not be eligible for parole until he is thirty-six.

The story of Hicks's crime lends substance to the commonly held view that the number of violent juvenile crimes is increasing and that the perpetrators of such crimes are getting younger. In recent years, the media have repeatedly reported shocking incidents of extreme violence committed by minors—even by preteens. Adding to the horror of these accounts is the fact that the perpetrators are often described as having no conscience, capable of killing over relatively trivial issues—such as a disrespectful look or an article of clothing—or even for no discernible reason at all. The bewilderment many citizens feel in the face of such stories is reflected in the words spoken to Hicks by his judge, Joan Weber, at his sentencing: "The thing that is incomprehensible about this case is how a boy of fourteen years of age can have so much hate and anger inside and so little regard for human life that you took this young man's life over a lousy pizza."

Along with media stories of youth violence, statistics also suggest a rise in juvenile crime. The FBI and the Department of

Justice point out that while the overall crime rates have remained fairly steady in recent years, the arrest rates for juveniles accused of violent crimes have risen dramatically. In addition, experts contend that a growing population of adolescent males will lead to a wave of crime in the early years of the twenty-first century. "America is a ticking violent crime bomb, and there is little time remaining to prepare for the blast," the Council on Crime in America warns.

Some observers argue that the extent of the juvenile crime problem has been exaggerated. For example, media critic Mike Males contends that sensationalistic coverage of the issue by the news media has led the public to believe the problem is worse than it actually is. Others, including Barry Krisberg, president of the National Council on Crime and Delinquency, question the reliability of statistics that suggest an increase in juvenile crime. However, the popular perception of a rising tide of youth violence persists, and many politicians, justice officials, and citizens have called for strong law-enforcement policies designed to combat juvenile crime. Measures that have been proposed or enacted include curfews to keep juveniles off the streets and out of trouble, military-style boot camps for first-time offenders, and elimination of the secrecy that surrounds juvenile justice proceedings.

One reform that has become increasingly popular is the practice of transferring juveniles to adult courts and institutions. Numerous states have lowered to thirteen or fourteen the age at which juveniles can be waived into adult courts and subject to adult sentences. Advocates of this approach argue that the juvenile justice system was established to respond to the relatively minor offenses, such as truancy and joyriding, typically perpetrated by youths in the past. In order to protect society from the more serious, violent crimes committed by some of today's juveniles, critics of the system assert, stronger punishments are required than those meted out by the juvenile courts. In defending the decision to try Hicks as an adult, Paul Pfingst, the district attorney for San Diego County, said, "No community can celebrate prosecuting fourteen-year-olds as adults for murder, but it's something we have to do because of the types of crimes they're committing. I don't know that there's an alternative but to hold them responsible by adult standards." Supporters argue that imposing harsh sanctions on juveniles—locking Tony Hicks up for twenty-five years, for example—sends the message that such behavior will not be tolerated and thereby deters other young people from committing similar acts.

The practice of transferring juveniles to adult courts is criticized on several grounds. Many critics contend that this approach is ineffective because juveniles are generally given lighter sentences in adult courts than in juvenile courts. Others insist that imposing harsh sentences on juveniles as a deterrent is futile because deterrence does not work on teenagers. According to James Alan Fox and Glenn Pierce of Northeastern University, "Trying juveniles as adults in order to incarcerate them longer . . . cannot be counted on for dissuading kids from the temptations and thrill of street crime. . . . Teens who are attracted to crime will always turn a deaf ear to deterrence." Still other opponents maintain that incarcerating juveniles in adult institutions is likely to traumatize them and teach them to be brutal criminals. According to Sarah Glazer, a freelance writer who specializes in social policy issues, sending juveniles to adult prisons "means sending them to schools for crime or handing them over to adult sexual predators."

Critics of the law enforcement approach argue that society should strive to reform delinquent juveniles rather than transferring them to adult courts and prisons. Supporters of the juvenile justice system maintain that its original mission was not to punish or deter criminals but to rehabilitate and nurture children in trouble. This can best be accomplished, they contend, by programs that provide education, job training, and therapy for psychological problems and drug addiction—programs that are less likely to be available to juveniles in adult institutions.

At his 1996 sentencing hearing, Tony Hicks told the judge, "I'll be a better person. I won't mess up. I want to hold my mom as tight as I can and beg her to take me out of jail." Some people believe that young offenders such as Hicks should indeed be treated as juveniles and helped to become better persons. Others insist that in order to protect the public from harm, killers—no matter what their age—must be severely punished and removed from society. Whether juveniles should be tried and sentenced as adults is among the issues discussed in *Juvenile Crime: Opposing Viewpoints*, which contains the following chapters: Are Juvenile Crime and Violence Increasing? What Causes Juvenile Crime and Violence? What Factors Contribute to Gang-Related Juvenile Crime? How Can Juvenile Crime Be Combated? Contributors to this anthology grapple with the various challenges posed by the problem of crime and violence committed by society's youngest members.

Are Juvenile Crime and Violence Increasing?

Juvenile
Crime

Chapter Preface

Shocking reports of violent crimes committed by juveniles seem to have become commonplace. For instance, in September 1994, eleven-year-old Robert Sandifer Jr. was shot in the head by teenage fellow gang members in Chicago. At the time of his death, Sandifer was being sought by police for the shooting death of a fourteen-year-old girl. One month later, also in Chicago, two boys dropped five-year-old Eric Morse from a fourteenth floor window because he refused to steal candy for them. In early 1996 in California, a six-year-old boy beat and kicked a four-week-old infant nearly to death during a burglary.

These stories fuel the widespread belief that violent juvenile crime is on the rise. This perception is further reinforced by statistics. Between 1985 and 1994, according to the Department of Justice, juvenile arrests increased 150 percent for murder, 103 percent for weapons law violations, 97 percent for aggravated assault, and 57 percent for robbery. While the majority of those arrested are males, arrest rates for female juveniles have also increased. Statistics from the National Center for Juvenile Justice for 1993 indicated that arrest rates for females between the ages of ten and eighteen rose 23 percent over the previous four years.

However, some commentators argue that reports of an increase in juvenile crime are unfounded. For example, Mike Males, author of *The Scapegoat Generation: America's War on Adolescents*, maintains that the media have created the impression that the problem of teen violence is worse than it actually is. Due to sensationalistic news coverage of the issue, says Males, "the average American adult believes that youths commit 43 percent of all violent crime in the U.S., three times the true figure of 13 percent."

Others question the validity of the statistical evidence of a rise in juvenile crime. Michael A. Jones and Barry Krisberg, authors of *Images and Reality: Juvenile Crime, Youth Violence, and Public Policy*, contend that arrest rate statistics exaggerate the problem. "Arrest statistics represent the *number of juveniles* arrested for violent crime—not the *number of violent crimes* committed by young people," they point out. Despite their high arrest rates, Jones and Krisberg insist, juveniles are no more likely to engage in violent crime than members of other age groups.

Some public policy experts warn that in the near future a growing population of adolescents will result in a wave of teenage crime. Other commentators claim that this threat is exaggerated. The extent of the problem of juvenile crime is the topic of the following chapter.

"Not long ago, kids were considered hopelessly delinquent when they skipped a day of school. . . . Today, many juveniles sell drugs, rape, rob, and shoot to kill."

Juvenile Crime and Violence Are Increasing

Margaret O. Hyde

While juvenile delinquency is hardly new to the United States, recent years have been marked by growing news coverage and public concern about the problem. In the following viewpoint, children's book author and former science teacher Margaret O. Hyde argues that juvenile crime is rising at an alarming rate. Citing statistics that link teenagers to weapons, sexual assault, and murder, she contends that juvenile crime increasingly involves younger children and intensifying brutality.

As you read, consider the following questions:

1. What juvenile crime statistics does Hyde cite? What sources does she give for these figures?
2. Why, according to Hyde, are many adults moving away from the cities?
3. What is the difference between juvenile delinquency in rural environments and in urban environments, in the author's opinion?

About 2.3 million persons under the age of eighteen are arrested by law enforcement agencies in the United States each year, according to the Office of Juvenile Justice and Delinquency Prevention. There are far more murders, rapes, and robberies by young people than in the past. The number of arrests of persons under the age of eighteen for violent crimes increased 62 percent between 1986 and 1991. Not all such crimes resulted in arrest, but there are other indicators of an increasing and changing crime scene among the young. For example, a 1993 survey by the National School Safety Council reports that 100,000 students across the country bring guns to school each day. Some of these students say that they do so for self-protection, but even their guns can cause tragedy.

Consider the case of a student, who reached in his backpack for a book, accidentally discharged his gun and killed a classmate. In one recent year, the increase in the number of guns confiscated from students in the Los Angeles Unified School District was 86 percent. Since 1965, the arrest rate for juveniles charged with violent crime has more than tripled.

Not only is the number of violent crimes increasing, the age of the offenders is decreasing. Ten-year-olds break into neighbors' houses; a pair of twelve- and fifteen-year-olds tie a man to a tree and set him on fire; a twelve-year-old murders a classmate in a fight over a baseball. These are just a few examples that illustrate the changing nature of juvenile crime.

Dangerous Games

In 1994, homicide was the third-leading cause of death for elementary and middle school children. In *Saving Our Kids from Delinquency, Drugs and Despair*, Falcon Baker suggests that crime is no longer a young man's game; it's getting to be child's play. Games of cops and robbers are now played with real guns, not toys.

Consider the games some teens play today in areas that are considered safe. Stealing cars is one. In a wealthy suburban area where the odor of burned rubber permeates the air on Saturday nights, citizens complain that teens have etched eights and doughnuts on the asphalt roads with the tires of their stolen cars. These kids lead less dangerous lives than many in urban areas, but they, too, seem unconcerned about the risk of dying. To them, the risk of dying in a car crash adds to the thrill of car theft. Some of their friends are held in jails after injuring or killing people who happened to be in the way. But most of these teens feel that it will not happen to them.

"Carjacking" is a new name for an old, but popular, teen crime. The players in this violent game steal a car by threatening the driver with a gun, forcing him or her to get out of the car. These thieves drive away while the owners of the cars stand in the street in a state of shock. Many carjackers act in daylight in places as crowded as a supermarket parking lot. In one case, the ejected driver was caught in the car door and carried along, her body bumping along the road as the car sped forward. People have been killed for resisting, or just for not getting out of their cars fast enough.

More Senseless and Violent

Although there have always been crimes by juveniles that appear to lack a motive, there seem to be more senseless crimes. For example, young people tried to set fire to homeless men sleeping in subway stations as many as twenty-two times in 1992. In these crimes, no one takes anything of value; there is nothing to take. The victims all appeared to be strangers to their torturers. One fire setter explained that he and his friends were playing near a man who was sleeping in the subway and they accidentally spilled some of their rum on him. Then they threw matches at him and when his blanket caught fire, they ran. Two other homeless men, who happened to come along soon after the fire started, threw themselves on the man and smothered the flames. They called the police, and ran after the boys. At the police station, the boys were charged with assault and attempted murder. They gave no good reasons for the attempts, although the fun of it was suggested as a motive.

Almost everyone agrees that many young criminals are becoming more violent. The number of murderers under the age of eighteen has climbed 93 percent since the 1980s. Murder is more common among today's children, many of whom are in trouble because of the violence around them. The Children's Defense Fund, a nonprofit organization supported primarily by foundations, corporate grants, and individual donations, reports that two children under the age of five are murdered in America each day. In the same short period of time, about 7,000 children are reported abused or neglected. Many more cases are not reported.

"Children in Crisis"

Growing up in America today is different for most young people than it was for their parents. Fear of violence and crime seems to be everywhere, from the mean streets of large cities to the halls of suburban and rural schools. Teenage boys, who once fought over their places in the drug market, now shoot so readily that the reasons may be only sneakers, leather jackets, or insults. Bystanders are caught in the cross fire of drug wars and people can be shot just because a young person feels like killing someone. Some kids have become so desensitized to shooting that they laugh about it. On the streets in many cities, "doing time" is a badge of honor.

Many adults are not, or do not want to be, aware of what is happening to today's children. They move farther from the cities, believing they can escape the problems of children in trouble. But even conservative magazines, that usually devote their pages more to business than social problems, are printing articles about today's "children in crisis." For example, in one issue of *Forbes* magazine, boys and girls from different cities talk about violence, hopes, cops, racism, drugs, school, and family. Others talk about juvenile homicide, suicide, and abuse.

Reprinted by permission: Tribune Media Services.

The Committee for Economic Development reflects the views of corporate America when it states publicly that it is concerned about whether or not children of today will have sufficient education, motivations, and undamaged brains to provide the needs of tomorrow's labor force.

From Fists to Guns

In addition to being more numerous and more serious, crimes by and against the young have changed in character. Boys used to settle arguments with their fists; now they settle them with guns. Gang members were once armed with zip guns; now they carry machine guns. Not long ago, kids were considered hopelessly delinquent when they skipped a day of school, stole an apple from the grocer, broke a window, or went joyriding one evening in the family car without permission. Today, many juveniles sell drugs, rape, rob, and shoot to kill. . . .

Large numbers of kids in poor areas feel that they have nothing to lose. Too many are growing up with a lack of feelings. They grow up unable to trust, love, and make meaningful relationships with other people. Many have been abused and will abuse their children.

Many of today's young already resort to drugs and brutality in an effort to get a sense of their own existence and to numb the deadness inside. Suppose a child lives in ten different homes before he starts kindergarten. He is farmed out to relatives, until they have no more room for him. Then he goes into foster care, and he is moved three times in one year. He always seems unhappy, refuses to abide by family rules, and never seems to develop a sense of attachment to any adult. Foster mothers of such children often complain that they seem like sticks when picked up. They do not throw their arms around their mothers when they are hugged, the way most children do. They remain aloof, and even many of those who are lucky enough to live with firm but loving foster mothers may go through life without feeling the emotions necessary to find love and happiness. Even though they try drugs and crime to feel alive, they feel no guilt.

No Simple Answers

Consider the case of three boys who raped a woman in a park. One, during questioning at the police station, said he was the good guy because he put her pocketbook under her head to make her more comfortable. He saw nothing wrong in what he had done. He, and many like him, will continue to prey on the public and to commit serious violent crimes. Attempts to rehabilitate them appear futile. This boy and thousands like him are in trouble, and the search is on for solutions that will help prevent the increase in the number of unattached, unfeeling children who are creating such terror. There are no simple answers, but there may be ways to help prevent many such problems.

The fear of violence by the young is changing the lives of people everywhere. In a world where the young have easy access to guns and no access to the American dream of success, anyone can be the victim of a shoot-out. Many thirteen-year-olds have attended more funerals for their friends than for grandparents. No wonder many young adults are pleading with political leaders and the general public to address some of the causes of violent crime: drugs, poverty, guns, and a value system that seems to make no sense. They plead for a new look at an antiquated juvenile justice system that is overwhelmed with cases and sometimes sends young people back to the streets with more desire and ability to break the law than before they entered the system.

What kind of system can cope with today's world in which many children have nightmares in the daytime, have mothers on crack, are abused by their natural parents, go to bed hungry, don't know their fathers, and who may die from gunshot wounds before they reach their tenth birthday? What can help kids who are growing up without love or affection, without beliefs, with no value for life? What can be done to make progress toward giving children a healthy and fair start in life?

According to the Honorable Charles D. Gill of Litchfield, Connecticut, the nation is in grave danger because of its benign neglect of its only real national treasure—its children. Many young people agree and they are looking for ways to make a difference in their world where violent death is the second leading cause of death for boys and more than four out of ten girls become pregnant at least once in their teens.

Whether out of compassion for others or concern for the world of tomorrow, there is a call to action. Ideas about how to keep kids out of trouble with the law differ. Some people believe that getting tougher with delinquents will help to break the cycle of violence and crime. While many people see delinquency as a result of poverty, racial discrimination, children having children, changes in family structure, poor health, illiteracy, lack of hope, and an environment of drugs and violence, they are searching for solutions. An increasing number of advocates are pushing for rights for kids, citing the many cases in which the young suffer from parental abuse and have no way out of their terrible situations.

Little Prisons

According to Judge David B. Mitchell, associate judge of Baltimore, Maryland, City Circuit Court, "It is of no value for the court to work miracles in rehabilitation if there are no opportunities for the child in the community and if the child is simply going to return to the squalor from which he or she came."

Judge Mitchell believes that most juvenile institutions are simply little prisons where inmates make contacts for future criminal activities. "For one of the first times in our Nation's history," he says, "we have a permanent underclass of poor black, white and Hispanic kids. These kids see no opportunities. They reside in intense, comprehensive poverty, have inadequate housing and educational systems that do not function. Until we deal with the environment in which kids live, whatever we do in the courts is irrelevant."

Many rural kids are in trouble, too. "A higher rate of kids in rural environments use tobacco, and alcohol in binge drinking, than kids in urban environments. Unless we recognize that substance abuse affects all of America and start attacking the broad scope of the problem, the juvenile court, the criminal court, and all courts will be irrelevant. All we shall be is conductors on the railroad to prison."

Unless there is increased awareness of what is happening in the world of juvenile crime, there is little hope for solutions through prevention. Even though progress in the war on juvenile crime may be measured in inches, you may be able to make a small difference.

"The 10-year trend in arrests for violent crimes . . . does not suggest that youth violence is any more out of control today than it was a decade ago."

Juvenile Crime and Violence Are Not Increasing

Michael A. Jones and Barry Krisberg

Public perceptions that juvenile crime is on the rise, both in terms of frequency and violence, result from misleading statistics, according to the National Council on Crime and Delinquency's senior researcher Michael A. Jones and president Barry Krisberg. In actuality, the authors argue, teens are committing fewer violent crimes than in previous decades and at rates disproportionately low for their segment of the population.

As you read, consider the following questions:

1. What do Jones and Krisberg consider a key difference between the FBI's Uniform Crime Report and the U.S. Justice Department's National Criminal Victimization Survey?
2. According to the authors, how can arrest statistics create an impression of exaggerated rates of juvenile crime?
3. How do "cleared" arrests, according to Jones and Krisberg, differ from the arrest statistics reported by the FBI?

Crime has become a major focus of public attention. Americans now view their world as an increasingly dangerous place to live, and fear of crime may be at an all-time high. Stories of drug abuse, sex crimes and violence routinely lead off our local news programs. Crime stories all too often capture newspaper headlines. Virtually every night television takes us into the front seat of a police car to witness firsthand crime scene after crime scene. In the comfort of our living rooms we are presented with re-creations of heinous unsolved crimes. These "virtual reality" crime shows leave us angry, afraid and somehow inexplicably entertained. But are we really less safe than we were 10 or 20 years ago, or do we just feel less safe? The facts suggest the latter.

While it is certainly true that our society suffers from too much violence, it is essential that we accurately review current crime trends if we are to develop rational policies. Policy choices are now being debated that will have far-reaching implications for our children and our communities. The purpose of this viewpoint is to inform the youth crime debate by answering the following questions:

- What are the actual trends regarding juvenile crime?
- Has violent crime by juveniles increased dramatically? . . .

Trends in Juvenile Crime and Youth Violence

There are two sources of information, provided by the federal government, which track crime trends in the United States. The Federal Bureau of Investigation (FBI) produces its annual Uniform Crime Report (UCR), providing estimates of arrests and crimes reported to police. The U.S. Justice Department also conducts an annual National Criminal Victimization Survey based on interviews of thousands of households across the country. The victimization survey picks up crimes not reported to police.

The Justice Department's victimization data indicate that overall levels of crime have actually fallen since 1973. Levels of violent crime in 1992 did not differ significantly from those recorded in 1981 and 1982. Rates of theft, larceny and household crimes were at their lowest levels since the government began conducting victimization surveys in 1973.

The FBI's UCR data provide us with the only measure of changes in the nation's murder rates. While the United States has a very high murder rate compared to other industrialized countries, this rate has not fluctuated much since 1973 according to the FBI. The current rate of 9.3 per 100,000 population is nearly identical to the rate of 9.4 per 100,000 recorded in 1973.

There were just over 14 million arrests in the United States in 1992—2 million more than in 1982. *During this ten-year period the contribution to this pool of total arrests by persons under the age of 18 years has actually declined.* Whereas 16 percent of total arrests in 1992 involved juveniles, in 1982 juveniles comprised 18 percent of all arrests. Looking at the most serious crimes, the same pattern emerges. Between 1982 and 1992 the proportion of total arrests for serious crimes attributed to juveniles decreased from 31 percent to 29 percent. During this same period, arrests of adults for serious crimes increased at a rate three times that for juveniles (5 percent for juveniles versus 15 percent for adults).

The vast majority of juveniles arrested in America are arrested for property crimes and other less serious offenses—not crimes of violence. In 1992, arrests for property offenses, particularly burglary and larceny, represented 85 percent of all arrests of juveniles for serious crimes. Well over half of violent arrests of juveniles in 1992 were for aggravated assault charges, with robbery and aggravated assault representing 93 percent of all juvenile violent crime arrests. Indeed, the most serious crimes of murder and rape represented only 7 percent of all juvenile violent arrests in 1992. Murder and rape combined represented less than half of one percent of all juvenile arrests in the United States in that same year.

Youth Arrested for Violent Crimes

Much of today's "crisis" is based on the perception that youth violence has gotten much worse in recent years. The 10-year trend in arrests for violent crimes, however, does not suggest that youth violence is any more out of control today than it was a decade ago. Juvenile arrests for violence increased by 45 percent between 1982 and 1992, but this increase was characteristic of violent crime arrests in general (adult arrests increased by 41 percent during that same period). In 1982, juveniles represented 17.2 percent of arrests for violent crimes, and by 1992 the proportion had increased by less than half of one percent to 17.5 percent. Between 1982 and 1992, the proportion of the youth population in America arrested for violent crimes increased from 0.3 percent to 0.5 percent.

While many lament the crisis of violence and juvenile crime, a closer look shows that recent increases in juvenile violent arrest rates are actually below historical trends. In fact, since 1965 the trend in arrest rates of juveniles has been consistently punctuated by a series of increases, decreases and plateaus. Overall, however, during the decade of the 1970s the increase in arrest rates for violent crimes for persons under the age of 18 years was actually double the increase recorded during the 1980s. According to the most recent figures reported by the FBI, the nation's serious and violent crime rate is declining in the 1990s.

Widely reported arrest rate statistics may exaggerate the problem of youth violence. FBI arrest statistics represent the *number of juveniles* arrested for violent crime—not the *number of violent crimes* committed by young people. Arrest statistics are, in large part, a reflection of policing policies and often tell us little about the actual amount of crime being committed. For example, if police arrest five juveniles in connection with a drive-by killing, this will appear in FBI arrest statistics as five homicide arrests, not one murder. This phenomena helps explain part of the difference between victimization and arrest rate trends.

Most Kids Are Not Criminals

Percentage of young people who get arrested

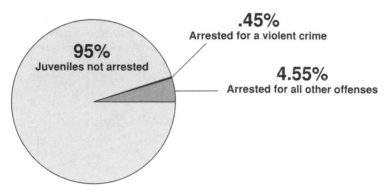

95%
Juveniles not arrested

.45%
Arrested for a violent crime

4.55%
Arrested for all other offenses

Source: National Center for Juvenile Justice, data for 1992.

Scholastic Update, September 15, 1995.

If one examines the proportion of crimes reported to law enforcement which are actually cleared by arrests of juveniles—a better measure of the amount of crime attributable to juveniles—a different picture emerges. Police clear or solve an offense when at least one person is arrested, charged with commission of the offense, and turned over to the court for prosecution. Juveniles consistently account for a smaller proportion of arrests cleared than arrest rate statistics would indicate.

While juveniles accounted for about 16 percent of total arrests in 1992 and 17.5 percent of all arrests for violent crime, they accounted for only about 12.5 percent of violent crimes cleared by arrests in that year. In other words, the proportion of violent crimes attributable to juveniles, as measured by the number of crimes cleared by law enforcement, is actually lower than the proportion of youth in the U.S. population and is well below the total number of reported arrests of juveniles for violent crimes.

The proportion of all property, serious and violent crimes cleared by arrest of persons under 18 years continues to be below levels reported in 1972. Based on these clearance data, it would appear that juveniles are arrested disproportionately for property offenses but are arrested for violent crimes at rates below the proportion of young people in the nation's population.

Differences between arrest and clearance rates are caused in large part by the greater tendency of juveniles to commit crimes in groups; this distorts the FBI arrest statistics and, therefore, overstates levels of juvenile violence. For instance, information published by the FBI suggests that the younger the offender, the greater the proportion of offenses committed in groups. In 1990, groups composed only of teenagers were responsible for between 35 and 47 percent of all multiple-offender attempted and completed violent crimes of rape, robbery and assault—a percentage that is more than twice that for offenders in their 20s and six times that for offenders 30 years of age or older.

"Where do I feel the most unsafe? Honestly? School."

Juvenile Violence Is a Serious Problem in the Schools

Merrica Turner

Violent crime in the schools affects parents and educators, but students tend to be the ones confronted most directly. According to student Merrica Turner, every day high school students face an environment characterized by shootings and public restrooms that are used as drug lairs. The lack of safety she felt at her former school was so great, she argues, that she opted for home study. Turner insists that her experience is not an isolated case but an illustration of the crime and violence that have infiltrated schools everywhere.

As you read, consider the following questions:

1. What type of institution does Turner compare schools to?
2. According to the author, why do students join crews or gangs?
3. In Turner's opinion, what provokes teens to start fights or commit drive-by shootings?

From "School Violence: Terror in the Halls" by Merrica Turner, *Report Card*, vol. 1, no. 1, January 1995; © Center for the Study of Popular Culture, 1995. Reprinted by permission.

If someone were to ask you to name a place where you feel safest, where would it be? And if you were asked where you feel unsafe, where would it be? Everyone has their problems at home, but that's where I feel safest—at home, in my house, with the people I love and who love me. Where do I feel the most unsafe? Honestly? School. And now I'm out of there—I'm in home study now. But I was there long enough to know just how bad things are.

I always thought that I could and should feel safe at school. But I never did. This was not one of those "inner-city" schools you read about in the papers or see on the nightly news. We're talking about the suburbs—Southern California's San Fernando Valley—the place everyone went to escape urban blight and crime.

Human Warehouses

The little red schoolhouse of legend is no more. When you go to my old school, the first thing you notice is the building's need for a paint job. Some of the floor tiles are dull and cracked. Generally, the place has a dark and depressing feeling, more like a reformatory than a place where learning takes place.

Some schools don't look so bad. Others have passed the point of no return. At Birmingham High School in Encino, California, blue tarps are hung around the playing fields to prevent outsiders from getting targets and being able to shoot in. There are bars on the windows to keep things from disappearing. Security is everywhere. They are usually retired folks in blue jackets who look like volunteers from the PTA. Some ride bikes. Some carry walkie-talkies. . . .

Some of the schools with open campuses have drug dealers driving right up to the front doors. Kids wander on and off campus at will, passing through the metal detectors. The grounds are littered with used condoms. The kids at one school are fond of one brand with Mickey Mouse ears on them. This isn't the kind the school distributes, though.

Bathrooms are unusable. They have become lairs for dope-peddlers, who go there to smoke or shoot up. Most of the bathrooms are locked up for lack of adequate security, and sanitation is almost nonexistent in those that remain open. I know of one school where the principal cleans the bathrooms. Maybe that's why there is only one bathroom open at a time. She doesn't have time to clean them all. The bathrooms are so bad that some boys actually urinate outside rather than endure the stench inside. The girls have no choice but to wait.

Some of the multi-level schools have elevators. Most of them have been closed off or dismantled because they had been so badly vandalized or taken over by drug dealers. Those remain-

ing are kept locked or restricted to staff members and the handi-
capped.

The schools I know are like human warehouses—punitive
type reformatories. These are supposed to be some of our better
suburban schools with the higher SAT scores and the bright
kids. It just so happens that the bright kids in one of the area
magnet schools spend a lot of time watching videos. At my old
school, they are watching the O.J. Simpson trial for civics. All
they have to do for homework is switch on the TV.

One of the top scholastic schools in the San Fernando Valley,
Taft High School, is also one of the most dangerous. In 1994,
sometime during winter semester, there was a guy caught hiding
out in the girls' bathroom. He had just shot at somebody. I guess
that's another reason for keeping the bathrooms locked. . . .

Turf Wars

Does something bad always have to happen to prove a point? I
guess so. In 1994, a student at one Valley high school didn't feel
safe, so he carried a loaded handgun with him at school. And
one day, during one of the passing periods, when the hallways
were packed with students going to their next class, he accidentally dropped his gun. It went off, killing an innocent teenager.
After that, the school installed metal detectors.

Gangs and crews are a big problem in school. The difference
between a gang and a crew is a gang has more banger types—
you know, *bang, bang* like a gun—while crews are basically tag-
gers. Crews just go out and mess stuff up with paint. They don't
really shoot people; they mostly fight.

Turf is everything. Every day teens approach other teens with
the question, "Where are you from?" If they are from a rival
crew or gang, you can bet there's going to be a fight. Somebody
might be stabbed or shot just for giving what some other guy
considers a wrong answer.

Most kids are in some kind of gang or crew because they are
afraid to be alone. Even if you aren't in a gang or crew, you usually have friends who are, and sometimes that causes you trouble. Almost every gang or crew has rivals, and that leads to conflicts. If one member has a problem with someone, then all the
members have that problem.

School violence is a problem for everybody—teachers, school
staff, parents *and* students. Some teachers really do try hard and
seem to care about the kids learning something and making
something of their lives. But most of them just want to get
through the day and go home. Some seem like they would prefer not to speak to, much less see, their students.

Can you honestly say that you can learn something in an at-
mosphere where you are so afraid and you feel like you are an

imposition just for being there? I know I couldn't and that's one of the reasons why I got into home study. Violence isn't exclusive to the high schools, either. Nowadays, the elementary and junior high school kids believe that carrying a gun or a shank, or fighting, are the only ways to feel secure.

A 10- or 11-year-old walking around strapped in order to feel safe is pretty sick, but it happens. It's hard for me to imagine what these kids are thinking. But I know that when I was in junior high the kids acted like they were my age now. They feel like they need to be protected, so they buy guns. It's not too much of a challenge. A teenage boy who lived down the street from me sold guns. I know about five other people who sell them.

Wasserman, © 1990, Boston Globe. Distributed by Los Angeles Times Syndicate. Reprinted with permission.

Girls buy small handguns to carry in their purses. When it's dark and you're alone, there's a better chance that a situation might take place. Not too long ago, I pulled into a gas station late at night. My friend got out to buy a candy bar. Before he even got to the service station's market, three thugs approached him, put a gun to his head and demanded his money. He gave them what they wanted, and they got in their car and sped off.

There isn't much time to be a kid. You know how kids get into drinking and smoking and sex because it makes them feel "grown up"? Well, shooting somebody because you might have a petty disagreement, or joining a gang to be accepted among your peers or just to look "hard" is also a way to feel "grown up."

People are continually getting praised for violence. So kids start fights, or do drive-bys, or come to school strapped. . . . By doing these things, they hope to become Mr. Big Man on Campus, or prove they are hard. But they don't think about the damage they cause, or the grieving families left in their wake. . . .

Nothing Is Safe

Every day something happens. On one occasion, my friends and I were walking down the street. A car pulled up to where we were, and two guys jumped out and started chasing us. They had mistaken one of my friends for a member of an enemy crew. The two guys tackled my friend and began punching and kicking him, and threatened to kill him.

Then there was a party we went to one night. Parties are always opportunities for trouble. Everyone was having fun until some big guys came in, yelling out their gang name, terrorizing the people there and hitting the guests up for money. Then some guys looked at them wrong, and fights broke out all through the party. People had bottles broken over their heads, and just about anything people could grab was used as weapons. People began to panic and run, causing even more injuries. Three people had to go to the hospital, seriously hurt. I guess I should say that most of the time, people don't really hang around these parties.

Nothing is safe anymore. Before you can go to a party, you have to make certain what color is okay to wear. You have to find out what crews are going to be there, and decide whether it is safe to go. You can't even go down the street for a hamburger without checking everything out first. If some different gang or crew is there, you either don't go or you go on in and risk a fight.

I hear stories all the time about how teens have guns or knives pulled on them. Most teenagers, especially the males, feel like they have to be hard and show off. I think it is ridiculous that they feel the need to prove how hard they are to other teens, or maybe themselves, all the time.

If you rank out and show you aren't as hard as everyone thought, or maybe you don't say where you are from when you are getting hit up, you lose respect in the eyes of your peers. Personally, I think it's smarter to rank out when your life is on the line. The fights are about nothing more than who you know.

Nowhere to Go

Not long ago, some of my good friends went to a party. It wasn't really their crowd. My friends are the hip-hop, baggy type and the girl who was having the party was more the trendy, surfer type. When my friends arrived, they were immediately confronted. They stayed for maybe 10 or 15 minutes before they decided to leave. They went back to their cars to decide where to go next. After a while, the girl who was throwing the party came out and told them to leave. Now, my friends were parked about a block down from the house. They weren't loud and they weren't hurting anybody, but this girl still went off on them.

One of my friends said, "We're not messing anything up, and we'll leave as soon as we figure out where we're gonna go." That wasn't good enough. This girl went back in her house and got these football players from her school. They came outside and started talking trash to my friends. They left without incident, except for a few nasty words back and forth.

Some of my guy friends went to school with the football players. A week later, there was a carnival at some estates and all of my friends and the other people from the party were there. One guy walked up to my friends with a group of his own and told them they had to leave. One of my male friends replied, "What?" and the other guy repeated, "You guys have to leave." My friend asked why, and the guy replied that he lived there and didn't want my friends to be there.

This was a carnival where everybody was. My friend said, "Oh, you live right *here*?" pointing to the ground. "Yeah," the guy replied. My friends just laughed and said, "Okay, whatever." Then another guy grabbed my friend's gold chain and said, "Oh, this is real Mr. Big Man." My friend said they would leave when they figured out someplace else to go. The other guy turned and walked a few steps, and when my friend wasn't looking, he turned around and socked my friend in the face. It turned into a big fight. My other friends jumped in. My best girlfriend got hit in the jaw.

The guy who started the fight at the carnival has tried to start up with my friends at school, but they have stayed cool about it. When I think about it, my friends could have had this guy seriously hurt. Or they could have been hurt themselves. At school, if you defend yourself, you're as much to blame as the one who started the fight in the first place. You are supposed to stand there and let some guy beat on you. That's why it's safer to travel in a group.

A More Violent World

I'm told these are the best years of my life. I sure hope not. If these are the best years, then why are there so many teen suicides? What parents should say is "These *should* be the best years of your life." I guess that was because their teen years were so good.

What happened? Are these problems caused by the older generation? Or ours? Nobody wants to take the blame—things just happened this way. I don't see anyone standing up and taking responsibility for what is happening to our schools.

The violence in school isn't caused only by kids of certain races or from dysfunctional families. Everyone is involved. And it's not a matter of going to a bad hangout and getting into trouble. You could be anywhere. Unresolved conflicts in school more often than not get resolved with fists after school. Everyone thinks they have to act harder than everyone else. Everyone has to be tough.

I don't understand why the world now is much more violent than it was when my parents were in school. We have all of this new technology that was supposed to make the world better. But we have all of this increased hostility and hatred as well. Advanced technology shouldn't mean advanced violence.

What did our parents have that we don't? Or maybe the question is, why do we have more violence and hate than our parents did?

Everybody says, *Well, the world is so much more complicated now. Society has changed. We are a "multicultural" world.* That doesn't make sense. Technology was supposed to uncomplicate things. All the multicultural programs were supposed to make people understand each other better. What happened?

Sometimes it seems like there's no point in trying to change things. But I don't want this kind of world for my kids, and none of my friends do, either. If the violence continues, if the schools aren't straightened out, it's not just our future that will be taken away, but our kids' futures, too.

"Certain education initiatives may be working to remedy discipline problems and violent outbreaks at schools."

Juvenile Violence Is Not a Serious Problem in the Schools

Diane Aleem, Oliver Moles, and Jessica Portner

In Part I of the following two-part viewpoint, Diane Aleem and Oliver Moles present statistics to support their contention that violent incidents in the public schools are relatively rare. Moreover, they assert, the majority of delinquent acts are instigated by a very small minority of students. In Part II, Jessica Portner argues that students feel safer at schools than they have in the past, possibly due to the educational system's efforts to combat school violence and to teachers' efforts to build constructive relationships with students. Aleem and Moles are cochairs of the U.S. Department of Education's Office of Educational Research and Improvement Work Group on Goal Six. Portner is a staff writer for *Education Week*, a nonpartisan weekly newspaper published by the nonprofit foundation Editorial Projects in Education.

As you read, consider the following questions:

1. How many teachers reported being physically attacked in 1991, according to the survey cited by Aleem and Moles?
2. According to Portner, how many students reported a decrease in school violence in the 1996 study?

From *Review of Research on Ways to Attain Goal Six* by Diane Aleem and Oliver Moles (Washington, DC: Government Printing Office, 1993). Jessica Portner, "Some Students Report Feeling Safer at School," *Education Week*, February 28, 1996. Reprinted with permission.

Violence in schools is a shocking but rather uncommon event. For example, in a 1991 national survey only 2 percent of teachers reported being physically attacked and 8 percent threatened with injury in the previous 12 months. Serious discipline problems are more common. Nineteen percent of the teachers reported being verbally abused by a student from their school in the previous four weeks—a serious discipline problem but not a violent act as the term is used here. Physical conflict among students was seen as a serious or moderate problem by 28 percent of the teachers.

Accounts from adolescent students of being victims of violent acts in schools vary widely and the method of collecting information is probably a factor in these disparities. Four-to-six-month rates range from 2 percent assaulted based on a household survey of 12 to 19 year olds to 23 percent of eighth graders who had fought with another student based on school questionnaires although it is often hard to say who started fights and therefore who is the original assailant. Fear for personal safety in schools was a concern for 12–16 percent of students in these two studies with blacks and American Indians being twice as likely as whites to report not feeling safe at school.

A Few Students, Many Factors

Some antisocial behavior is fairly common among youth such as "exploratory" rebellious behavior. But a small proportion of students may be responsible for a large part of disciplinary referrals. For officially recorded crimes, over half are committed by only 6–7 percent of persons. Repeated antisocial behaviors among preadolescents such as fighting and being disruptive are strongly associated with later delinquency. Studies following students from the earliest grades show that teacher ratings of classroom disturbance, disrespect and impatience predict well different kinds of misbehavior and psychological problems in adolescence.

Misbehavior in school is affected by risk factors in the student and the environment. Males outnumber females three to one. Misbehaving youths display less academic competence, limited career goals, dislike of school, more delinquent friends, and less belief in school rules than their more conforming peers. They also demonstrate poor interpersonal and problem-solving skills, lack of deference to authority, and aggression. Peers often reject them.

Adolescents from lower socioeconomic status (SES) families commit more serious assaultive offenses in the community than youth from higher SES levels. Family factors strongly related to serious offenses include lack of parental supervision, indifference, rejection, and criminal behavior of parents. Contrary to common perceptions, divorce and separation by themselves play only a small part.

Violence also needs to be seen in relation to the community. Schools in neighborhoods with higher crime rates and fighting gangs have more violence as outside problems spill over into the school. In the above household study of teenage students 15 percent reported street gangs at their schools. Of these students 28 percent said there were fights between gang members at school at least once a month. More Hispanic (32 percent) than black (20 percent) than white students (14 percent) indicated the presence of gangs in their schools.

Safer than We Think

Is violence in schools as widespread as it seems? Our 1994 survey asked a representative sampling of the nation's school board members. Given the emphasis on violence in the press, our key findings come as something of a surprise:

. . . A respondent in a small community says, "Our school system has very few incidences of 'violence'—more on the order of fist-fights or scuffles." The reason? Principals enforce the conduct code immediately and involve parents in deliberations. Parents also have instilled a strong system of values in their children, he says. . . .

The majority of respondents overall perceive preschool and elementary intervention programs (55.4 percent), increased extracurricular programs (61.2), increased counseling services (59.2), peer mediation programs (52.6), and alternative school programs (58.6) to be effective. "Ours is a K–6 district," notes one respondent. "Rather than violence, we see an increase in disruptive behavior and inability to control impulsive reactions. Conflict-mediation/peer-mediation programs have had a positive effect on the youngsters.". . .

Overall results are encouraging. Despite newspaper headlines, our survey indicates that the picture is not as bleak as many imagine. The view from the school board is that students and staff are safe at school, and school districts are successfully implementing a wide variety of measures to keep them that way.

William Weisenburger, Kenneth E. Underwood, and Jim C. Fortune, *Education Digest*, May 1995.

The problem is not just in families and communities. From a large national study which helped launch the investigation of crime in schools, those schools with more male students, larger enrollments, larger classes, and junior highs (vs. senior highs) had more violence, as did those schools lacking strict and fair administration of discipline. And when students felt their classes did not teach them what they wanted to learn, did not consider grades important or plan to go to college, and felt they could not influence their own lives, more school violence also occurred.

More disorder also occurs when teachers think students should be punished severely for misbehavior, staff cannot agree on how to handle misbehavior or ignore it, resources for teaching are lacking, and rules are seen as unfair and not firmly enforced. More disorder occurs—even when schools similar in urban location, racial composition, socioeconomic status, and neighborhood crime are compared. Thus personal, family, community, school and classroom factors all play a part in violence occurring in schools. Efforts to reduce discipline problems and violence in schools need to consider these multiple sources of the problem.

II

Though national reports show that crime and violence among youths continue to increase, some students say schools are less violent than they were in 1994.

In a 1996 survey, 22 percent of students reported that violence in their schools had decreased in the past year; just 14 percent had reported such a decrease in an earlier poll done in 1994. In the 1996 survey, 21 percent reported an increase in violence, compared with 24 percent in 1994.

The survey has a margin of error of plus or minus 3 percentage points.

The Metropolitan Life Insurance Company poll, the third in recent years on violence in the public schools, was conducted from December 19, 1995, to February 2, 1996, by Louis Harris & Associates Inc. Researchers distributed questionnaires to 2,524 students in grades 7–12 in 48 states. The two earlier surveys included a 1994 poll of more than 1,000 parents and about 2,500 students. The results were published in *Education Week*.

In December 1993, Metropolitan Life released a survey of public school teachers, students, and police department officials. That report found that students generally felt less safe than teachers.

The new report is the first of four planned surveys focused exclusively on students.

Impact on Schools

The report says that the improvement in many students' perceptions about violence may show that certain education initiatives may be working to remedy discipline problems and violent outbreaks at school.

Another finding that school officials may find encouraging is the connection students made in the survey between teachers' attitudes toward their classes and an improved school environment.

Students who say their teachers treat them with respect are twice as likely as other students to report fewer fights, turf battles, and better relations among students.

"Kids can get positive social skills from a positive school environment," said Katherine Binns, a senior vice president at Louis Harris.

The message, Ms. Binns said, is that teachers who may feel discouraged by the many factors that contribute to social problems at school should understand that teachers can make a difference.

"Emphasis [is] on the violence young people commit and not on the institutionalized violence—the barbarity, if you will—that they have been raised with since birth."

Juveniles Are Unfairly Blamed for Increasing Crime and Violence

Susan Douglas

As news headlines announce violent crimes committed by juveniles, many sectors of society react with alarm to what they perceive as a rising trend in teenage brutality. In the following viewpoint, media reporter Susan Douglas argues that this concern is misguided and that many commentators are scapegoating adolescents rather than addressing the source of the problem. The greater evil, she contends, is not the criminal behavior of today's youth but the indifference of society toward the welfare of children and teenagers. Douglas writes the monthly column "Pundit Watch" for the *Progressive*, a monthly liberal newsmagazine.

As you read, consider the following questions:

1. What pattern characterizes news coverage of youth violence, according to Douglas?
2. According to Douglas, what is an example of the "institutionalized violence" experienced by America's children?
3. What does the author suggest as an alternative to the push for more stringent punishments for juvenile crime?

Susan Douglas, "Self-Righteous Kid-Bashing," *Progressive*, November 1993. Reprinted by permission from the *Progressive*, 409 E. Main St., Madison, WI 53703.

Of all the vacuous platitudes to spill forth from punditland, few are more hollow than the solemn announcement that a particular event is "a wake-up call for America." The 1992 Los Angeles "riots" were proclaimed such a wake-up call; so were the slayings of two Japanese exchange students in 1993; and so, the following three years, have been the murders of tourists in Florida. But as soon as the pundits feel they have done their duty by mouthing this cliche and advancing a series of solutions Joseph Stalin might admire, they hit the snooze alarm and go back to their dreamland where white men in suits, safely sequestered in posh and well-guarded office buildings, are the ones who most deserve our attention.

Criminal Coverage

Here's the typical pattern. An event occurs revealing, once again, the pathological strain of violence in America, made considerably more virulent by the insane proliferation of guns. Next, the media spotlight probes into the dysfunctional nature of the black family, the irremediable barbarism of black youth, and the utter hopelessness of reversing the trend, except for building more jails and hiring more police. Then it's on to asinine predictions about whether Yasser Arafat will or will not be killed by "his own people," or whether the passage of NAFTA [the North American Free Trade Agreement] will hurt Ross Perot's standing in the polls.

The dismissive—indeed, moronic and often vindictive—coverage of the terrifying rise of violence in America, especially in the lives of our nation's children, is itself nothing short of criminal. The pundits, most of whom are clueless about the status of children in America, spew a lot of superficial blather about "values" and two-parent families while failing to discuss even one concrete proposal that would help prevent kids beset by violence and poverty from turning into murderers.

In the wake of the latest murders in Florida, we see how such coverage urges white America to throw up its hands in despair and support completely reactionary, and often unconstitutional, politics. While emphasizing that black children need safer communities and a sense of hope about their futures, William Raspberry, on *Meet the Press*, also insisted that "White people cannot reach this group" and that there is nothing the Government can do about the current situation, except for imposing swifter and harsher punishments on youthful offenders.

This Week with David Brinkley devoted an entire show to "the barbarity" of murdering foreign tourists and the rise of "youth violence." Emphasis was on the violence young people commit and not on the institutionalized violence—the barbarity, if you will—that they have been raised with since birth. And a sound-

42

bite like "Maybe 80 percent of these crimes are blacks victimizing whites" only reinforces the racist myth that most black kids are criminals, and completely inverts the real power inequities between the races.

Every guest on the Brinkley show insisted that there was no role for the Federal Government to play in this crisis, but that solutions had to come from individuals and their communities. Yet these same experts urged vaguely that there be more "support" for inner-city families, especially for single mothers. How you "support" young mothers without the Federal Government financing quality low-cost child care, or providing incentives for private investment to create jobs in our inner cities, or making birth control and abortion cheap, if not free, and easily available, is beyond me.

Exacerbating the Problem

All the get-tough, more-cops-on-the-street, crack-down-on-crime hysteria only makes things worse. By patrolling the streets like an occupying army, the police teach inner-city youth that society is their enemy that they should hate. By locking more young offenders up, rather than attack the causes of violence, they help create disturbed, career criminals.

Erik Parsels, *New Unionist*, March 1994.

No one pointed out that nearly 22 percent of children under the age of eighteen live in poverty, and that poverty is more common for children than for any other age group. In the 1980s, while the number of U.S. billionaires quintupled, the number of children who fell into poverty increased by more than two million. Nor did anyone note that if we took the $160 billion or so we're spending on the S&L bailout, and directed it toward our public schools, child-abuse treatment programs, and health and nutrition programs for our kids, we might start getting somewhere.

Instead, we got some totally gratuitous—and worthless—sixties bashing, as when Isaac Fulwood, former chief of police of Washington, D.C., asserted that one big source of the problem is that people "were taught in the 1960s that . . . there is no right and wrong." Not only is this utter drivel, it gets us nowhere.

Not to be outdone, George Will insisted that the real problem is rhetorical, that "there [is] something in the very vocabulary of the therapeutic state of Florida that doesn't sound quite serious about crime" and that what we really need is "the language of punishment." Will would back up this sure-fire linguistic initiative with 150,000 to 200,000 more cops, advocating "the saturation of bad neighborhoods with good policemen." I guess it's easy to argue for a police state when you're white and rich, and have scrubbed from your disk the images of Rodney King being pummeled by some good ole boys in blue.

A Role to Play

Nina Totenberg seems to believe the Federal Government does have a role to play, and she uttered the two words that have been unutterable on the talk shows: gun control. Gordon Petersen, advancing one of the biggest pundit whoppers ever, said, "We've talked about gun control endlessly here, I don't know what you could say at this point." Excuse me, Gordon, you all *never* talk about gun control, as evidenced by Evan Thomas's staggering blooper that there are "200,000 guns" in circulation in America. Evan, would you please slide that decimal point over just a tad: the correct and horrendous figure is 200 *million* firearms in circulation, 60 to 70 *million* of them handguns, which kill fourteen children every day in this country. When are the other pundits going to follow Totenberg's lead, get some guts, and take on one of the great sources of evil in our country, the National Rifle Association?

This Week with David Brinkley would have done well to feature some other experts—the teenage editors of *Children's Express* and the young people they interviewed in *Voices from the Future*, a powerful collection of oral histories about growing up with violence in America. Someone from the Children's Defense Fund might have been able to squeeze in some specific policy proposals amid all the self-righteous kid-bashing. Yes, the murders of foreign tourists are savage and repugnant. But so are the childhoods that lead those kids to pull the trigger.

"Why are boys not even old enough to vote allegedly assaulting women with a hatefulness that seems to defy all reason?"

Juveniles Are Becoming Ruthless

Michele Ingrassia

Crimes committed by youths are becoming increasingly vicious, journalist Michele Ingrassia contends in the following viewpoint. Describing in detail the brutality of several attacks committed by teens during 1993, Ingrassia maintains that many youthful offenders take pride in their ruthlessness. Ingrassia is a general editor for *Newsweek*, a national weekly magazine.

As you read, consider the following questions:

1. What are two sources from which Ingrassia draws her statistics?
2. What does Ingrassia consider the "most overpowering" aspect of the Houston teenage murder suspects? What examples does she provide to illustrate her point?
3. What happens during a "feeding frenzy," according to the experts the author cites in the viewpoint?

Even for a society accustomed to daily reports from its urban war zones, this was a chilling tale. On a hot, steamy evening in late June 1993, police say, six members of Houston's Black N White gang gathered in an isolated area near the White Oak Bayou to down some beers and initiate two wanna-bes into their ranks—a macho ritual that demanded the newcomers fistfight the veterans. Around 11:30 p.m.—just after the induction ended and some members left—Jennifer Ertman, 14, and Elizabeth Peña, 16, set out from a pool party. They called home to say they were on their way. And then they took a deadly shortcut into the woods. Police say they stumbled onto the path of the still-pumped-up gang. "Let's get 'em," one allegedly urged. The nude bodies of the girls were found four days later; they had been raped repeatedly and strangled, one with a belt, the other with shoelaces. It was not enough. "To ensure that both of them were dead," a police spokesman said, "the suspects stood on the girls' necks."

The details of the killings stunned Houston and the rest of the nation. The viciousness of the attack near the remote railroad tracks was bad enough, but the cavalier attitude of the six 14- to 18-year-old suspects was even more disturbing. All six teens, police say, participated in the rapes and strangulations of the two young girls. Despite the serious charges, some of the suspects seemed to glory in their 15 minutes of fame. Once again, a sex crime has touched off grim questions: Why are boys not even old enough to vote allegedly assaulting women with a hatefulness that seems to defy all reason? And how can anyone so young snatch a life as casually as he might a car stereo?

Commonplace Sexual Aggression

Ever since the "wilding" spree in 1989, when a gang of New York City youths brutalized a woman jogger in Central Park, adolescent sexual aggression or violence seems more and more commonplace. In the spring of 1993, a group of California high-school jocks called the Spur Posse boasted their way onto the junk-TV circuit with brazen tales of how they kept score of the girls they had sex with. That June in Montclair, N.J., six boys, 13 to 16, were arrested on charges of sexual assault on a seventh-grade girl. And the following month New Yorkers were introduced to "whirlpooling" after police arrested two youths for allegedly assaulting a 14-year-old girl in a South Bronx pool. Typically, observers say, the "game" involves gangs of teenage boys who lock arms and move through public pools, surrounding girls and groping them under cover of the churning water. This time, several boys allegedly ripped off the girl's suit, and one inserted a finger into her vagina.

In a culture that allows young men to strut down the street wearing YOU STUPID BITCH T-shirts and to wade through city

46

pools, reportedly rapping "Whoomp, there it is" at females, the increase in adolescent violence is no illusion. Howard Snyder of the National Center for Juvenile Justice says that between 1988 and 1993 the number of murders committed by youths under 18 has skyrocketed by 85 percent. Federal Bureau of Investigation (FBI) figures show that while arrests for adult sex offenses rose by 3 percent between 1990 and 1991, the increase was three times as high for adolescents.

Youth Violence Hits a New Peak

By all accounts, violent crimes—homicide, rape, robbery, aggravated assault—are on the decline in the United States. Even so, there is an important reason for society to be concerned: America is experiencing a historically unprecedented epidemic of youth violence. Even as overall levels of violent crime have diminished since 1990, rates at which young people aged 14-18 have at tacked and been victimized by one another have increased dramatically. Both offending and victimization rates for this age group are now at historical peaks.

Mark H. Moore, *Jobs & Capital*, vol. IV, Winter 1995.

The violence hits hardest at the underclass, for whom aggression is a daily fact of life. Of course, as the Spur Posse and the New Jersey case prove, comfortable middle-class suburban youths are not immune. Michael Cox, head of a sexual-abuse treatment program at Texas's Baylor College of Medicine, calls the violent youthquake a "downward extension of the dysfunction we're seeing in society—with drug problems, guns, split-apart families."

Whether those were factors in the lives of the Houston suspects won't be known for a while—if ever. Officials have not even sorted out the backgrounds of all six boys. "He's probably the most hated person in Houston right now," attorney Donald Davis says of his client, Peter Anthony Cantu, 18, the alleged ringleader in the killings. Cantu comes from an intact family. He dropped out of school in 10th grade and ever since has worked with his father doing light construction. Like some of the others, he attended an alternative school for emotionally disturbed adolescents and students considered at high risk for landing in the juvenile-justice system. So far, defendant Derrick Sean O'Brien, 18, seems to bear the most visible scars of trouble. The product of a broken home, he was raised by his grandmother and no one knows who his father is, says Lon Harper, his court-appointed attorney. Harper says O'Brien was sexually abused by a male teacher and has attempted suicide several times.

Yet, to the public, the most overpowering image of the boys is their lack of remorse. One by one they seemed to spit in society's eye. "Hey, great! We've hit the big time!" defendant Raul Omar Villareal, 17, allegedly told O'Brien after hearing they might be charged with murder. Houstonians recoiled, too, at the realization that, a day before the slayings, O'Brien had appeared on a local TV program about gangs and, hoisting a beer, boasted: "Human life means nothing." Although the attorneys deny the boys are callous, even prosecutors are astonished. They are not alone. At a hearing on June 30, 1993, the suspects showed up in court with derogatory remarks scrawled on the backs of their tan jumpsuits, presumably by revulsed inmates at the Harris County jail. I'M A FAG, read a message on Cantu's uniform. I'M A BITCH was scribbled on O'Brien's.

Potent Mix

Youthful violence, of course, is not new. But some recent crimes seem to disregard even the barest of human boundaries. Richard Pesikoff, a Baylor College of Medicine psychiatrist for children and adolescents, calls the escalating mayhem a "Molotov explosive experience" fueled by a potent mix: aggression, drugs, alcohol, race and an ever-darker attitude toward women. The result: gang members spur each other downward, "encouraging each other to perform more and more heinous acts." Some experts blame the breakdown of families and their extended support networks. The gaping holes left by absent parents are too frequently filled by gangs—an often deadly bargain struck at a time when teens are naturally pushing away from home.

To Cox, it's "the rebel finding a cause": the gang gives members the identity and attention missing from the rest of their lives. The result can be deadly—what many call a "feeding frenzy" spurred by a gang leader who provides direction and sanction to the rest. Over the years, University of Pennsylvania criminologist Marvin Wolfgang says, research has shown that about 85 percent of juvenile offenses are committed in groups of two or more. And in a gang the conscience that normally would stop a healthy person from committing a crime is damaged or missing altogether. That's when gruesome acts can happen. The victim becomes dehumanized in the attacker's mind, Pesikoff says, and then "they are treated as a thing."

Such theorizing is small comfort for Connie Peña, the grandmother of one of the slain girls. "She used to say to me the world is OK, there weren't any bad people out there," Peña said in July 1993. "'No, Grandma,' she always told me when I described dangerous folks to her, 'they're not like that.'" It is an innocent faith—and one that makes the girls' deaths even more tragic.

Periodical Bibliography

The following articles have been selected to supplement the diverse views presented in this chapter. Addresses are provided for periodicals not indexed in the *Readers' Guide to Periodical Literature*, the *Alternative Press Index*, or the *Social Sciences Index*.

Jerry Adler	"Kids Growing Up Scared," *Newsweek*, January 10, 1994.
Rick Bragg	"Where a Child on the Stoop Can Strike Fear," *New York Times*, December 2, 1994.
Kathryn Casey	"When Children Rape," *Ladies' Home Journal*, June 1995.
Children's Voice	"Kids, Crime, and Common Sense: Reports Counter Media Assumptions," Winter 1995. Available from Child Welfare League of America, 440 First St. NW, Suite 310, Washington, DC 20001-2085.
Barbara Dority	"Anti-Crime Hysteria," *Humanist*, January/February 1994.
David Gelman	"When Kids Molest Kids," *Newsweek*, March 30, 1992.
Ted Gest and Dorian R. Friedman	"The New Crime Wave," *U.S. News & World Report*, August 29–September 5, 1994.
J. Hamilton	"It's a Jungle Out There," *Canada and the World*, January 1993.
Ronald Henkoff	"Kids Are Killing, Dying, Bleeding," *Fortune*, August 10, 1992.
Barbara Kantrowitz	"Wild in the Streets," *Newsweek*, August 2, 1993.
Adrian Nicole LeBlanc	"Falling," *Esquire*, April 1995.
Mike Males	"Bashing Youth: Media Myths About Teenagers," *Extra!* March/April 1994. Available from FAIR, PO Box 911, Pearl River, NY 10965-0911.
Scholastic Update	Shattered Youth: The Crisis of Teen Violence," February 11, 1994.
Joe Sexton	"Young Criminals' Prey Are Usually as Young: Portraits of Victims," *New York Times*, December 1, 1994.
Holly Sklar	"Young and Guilty by Stereotype," *Z Magazine*, July/August 1993.
Jennifer Vogel	"Throw Away the Key," *Utne Reader*, July 1994.
William Weisenburger, Kenneth E. Underwood, and Jim C. Fortune	"Are Schools Safer Than We Think?" *Education Digest*, May 1995.

What Causes Juvenile Crime and Violence?

Juvenile
Crime

Chapter Preface

Many theories are offered to explain why some juveniles commit acts of crime and violence. Suggested causes include the corrupting influence of violence in the popular culture—especially on television and in rap music; an abusive family environment; a neighborhood characterized by violence, poverty, or racial discrimination; an inadequate education system; a lack of community support; a lack of personal responsibility and moral values; a lenient juvenile justice system; and the existence of a genetic predisposition to violence. Commentators focus on these and other potential influences as they attempt to grapple with the complex social phenomenon of youth crime.

One possible cause of juvenile crime that has received significant attention in recent years is the increasing number of single-parent families. Many social critics argue that children from single-parent families—which are usually headed by women—are more likely than those from two-parent families to commit crimes. Boys from such families are especially at risk, these commentators maintain, because their homes lack the presence of an adult male to provide guidance and an example of mature, responsible conduct. According to Michael Tanner, the director of health and welfare studies at the Cato Institute, a libertarian research organization, "The boy in search of male guidance and companionship may end up in the company of gangs or other undesirable influences."

Others are less inclined to see single-parent families as a cause of juvenile crime. Reviewing the research on the relationship between single-parent families and juvenile crime, Kevin N. Wright and Karen E. Wright discovered that while some studies found evidence of a link between the two phenomena, others concluded that no such relationship exists. In addition, many people argue that although there is a link between single mothers and juvenile crime, the connection is not causal. These critics believe that the main cause of juvenile crime is poverty. The crime rate among juveniles from single-parent families is high, they insist, because single-parent families are more likely to be poor than are two-parent families.

The relationship between single-parent families and teenage delinquency is just one of the issues debated in the following chapter on the causes of juvenile crime and violence.

"Children who watched a lot of TV violence at 8 years of age have a higher propensity to commit violent crime by age 30."

Television Violence Contributes to Juvenile Crime

Mortimer B. Zuckerman

The impact of television violence on children has been debated since TV first arrived in the American living room. In the following viewpoint, Mortimer B. Zuckerman argues that concern over children's exposure to television violence is valid. According to Zuckerman, studies show that the more violent TV programs children watch, the more likely they are to commit violent crimes. He faults the television industry for failing to curtail the violence in their broadcasts and insists that decisive action must be taken to lessen children's exposure to violent programming. Zuckerman is chairman of and editor in chief for *U.S. News & World Report*, a national weekly newsmagazine.

As you read, consider the following questions:

1. What is TV an acronym for, in Zuckerman's opinion?
2. What does "common sense" dictate, according to Zuckerman?
3. In the author's opinion, who should be held responsible for proving or disproving the connection between TV violence and juvenile violence?

Mortimer B. Zuckerman, "The Victims of TV Violence," *U.S. News & World Report*, August 2, 1993. Copyright 1993, U.S. News & World Report. Reprinted with permission.

Do you despair at the sight of the youngster in a trance in front of the television set? You are not alone. With sets turned on in the inner city for 11 hours a day, with video, pay per view and multiplying cable channels, TV has become the closest and most constant companion for American children. It has become the nation's mom and pop, storyteller, baby sitter, preacher and teacher. Our children watch an astonishing 5,000 hours by the first grade and 19,000 hours by the end of high school—more time than they spend in class. The question more and more concerning parents, psychologists and public officials is this: What is all this viewing doing to them?

The Impact of TV Violence

The greatest impact is on preadolescent children who do not yet have the capacity to gauge what is real and what is not. To them, TV is a report on how the world really works. There may be a comic side to it. One Indiana school board had to issue an advisory that there is no such thing as the Teenage Mutant Ninja Turtles that the children had been crawling down storm drains to reach. But there is nothing amusing about the perception children gain from TV that violence is the easy solution to many problems, employed by good characters as much as bad and always leading to a happy ending.

The concern is that in later life, those conditioned to violence will intuitively continue to regard it as exciting, charismatic and effective. Consider how pervasive it is. By the age of 18, according to one estimate, a youngster will have seen 200,000 acts of violence on TV, including 40,000 murders. *TV Guide* looked at 10 channels on one normal 18-hour day and found 1,846 individual acts of violence—and every hour of prime time carries six to eight acts of violence. Violence has become normal, the Pied Piper to lure the vulnerable to a darker world.

The youthful world has become dramatically more violent. Consider this piece of anecdotal evidence turned up by CBS News: The seven top problems in public schools in 1940 were identified by teachers as talking out of turn, chewing gum, making noise, running in the halls, cutting in line, dress-code infractions and littering. By 1980, the seven top problems had been identified as suicide, assault, robbery, rape, drug abuse, alcohol abuse and pregnancy.

It is hard to avoid the judgment that TV, an acronym for too violent, has become an integral part of this problem. Research suggests that it increases physical aggression in children, such as getting into fights and disrupting the play of others. Does this increase in aggression contribute to the explosion of criminal violence? Many argue that it does. They point to studies such as one demonstrating that children who watched a lot of TV violence at

8 years of age have a higher propensity to commit violent crime by age 30, including the beating of their own children.

The Minimum Next Step

There are those who argue that TV violence is a cathartic rather than a stimulant. Indeed, precise malign connections may be difficult to prove. But common sense dictates that the effect cannot be good. Some 80 percent of Americans feel that TV violence is harmful to our society and that there is too much of it in our entertainment. The burden of proof should fall on those who continue to promote violence and use it as entertainment.

Reprinted by permission of Mike Thompson and Copley News Service.

The TV networks have made a concession by providing a rating system to alert viewers to impending violence. It is a gesture, but that is all it is. It identifies the violence but it does not remove it. It puts the onus on the parents—and parents do have a duty to protect their children from the brutalizing effect of nightly sluggings. But parents cannot do it all, given absences for work and for travel, that many children watch TV in their own rooms, and that the alert system excludes cartoons, cable, videos and so forth.

The alert system is no more than a beginning, a recognition but not a resolution. The minimum next step is to take advantage of the technical capacity to manufacture TV sets with a computer chip that will allow parents, unilaterally, to block off programs carrying the V rating—just as we now mandate sets to help the deaf. And with that should go an earnest effort by the creative controllers to take the V out of much more of their television. It is not a happy prospect that a commercial Big Brother could substitute for the Orwellian Big Brother.

"Repeated illustrations of violence and immorality are necessary to impart ethical lessons."

Television Violence Teaches Children Morality

Laurence Jarvik

Many people argue that television violence causes children to engage in violent behavior, including violent crime. In the following viewpoint, Laurence Jarvik contends that television programs frequently use violence to teach moral lessons. Comparing contemporary television shows to biblical stories, Jarvik insists that good cannot be taught unless evil—including acts of violence—is also depicted. Moreover, Jarvik asserts, television heroes often use violence for positive purposes, such as ensuring moral order. Jarvik is director of the Center for the Study of Popular Culture.

As you read, consider the following questions:

1. Why is it important to use "the moral factor" when measuring television violence, according to Robert Knight, as quoted by Jarvik?
2. Why is the finding that TV "good guys" commit more acts of violence than "bad guys" encouraging, in the author's opinion?
3. What institution does Jarvik credit for ensuring the moral integrity of films produced during Hollywood's Golden Age?

The Norwegian prime minister tried to blame a children's television program for the brutal murder of a 5-year-old girl by two other children, ages 5 and 6, in the city of Trondheim. *Mighty Morphin' Power Rangers* was taken off the air by Swedish television after Gro Harlem Bruntdland declared that free-market violence on television was responsible. Not negligent parents who failed to supervise the child's activities. Not the welfare state of which Bruntdland is the top official. Not the Scandinavian version of feminism, which has separated mothers from their children and caused a rising tide of illegitimacy. Not the decline in religious faith among Norwegians. Instead, Bruntdland blamed American cartoons—made in Japan!

Of course, Bruntdland was wrong. Within a few weeks Scandinavian television returned the *Power Rangers* to the air, noting that there was no evidence to link the program to the murders. That the prime minister's wild accusation was taken seriously in the first place shows the reduced stature of commonsense arguments in public debate over violence on television.

Good Violence vs. Bad Violence

No one would deny that what appears on television affects viewers. No one would deny that children should be protected from programming that is not age-appropriate. The best solution to the problem of television violence may be to reinforce the traditional institutions of church, family and neighborhood, which provide the moral armor against bad influences from other sectors of society. And such institutions depend on a moral order deeply rooted in faith rather than social science. Yet current debates over television often are conducted on a terrain that favors liberal social engineering.

This attitude reflects a view of the perfectibility of man, which tries to redefine crime, for example, as a medical problem rather than a moral failure, one of violence rather than of evil. But this view fails to make commonsense distinctions. There is good violence and there is bad violence. When Cain slew Abel, it did not have the same moral dimension as when David slew Goliath. Yet the social scientist would record both actions as "violent" in a content analysis of the Bible.

As Rene Girard commented regarding religious ritual in *Violence and the Sacred:* "The secret of the dual nature of violence still eludes men. Beneficial violence must be distinguished from harmful violence, and the former continually promoted at the expense of the latter. Ritual is nothing more than the regular exercise of 'good' violence."

Masterpiece Theatre provided a secular example of such ritual when it aired "Dandelion Dead," the story of a serial poisoner who gets caught, tried, convicted and hanged. The hanging was the triumph of good over evil—a violent triumph. In fact, the violence of the hanging was greater than the violence of the poisonings. Yet the poisonings were the crime, and the hanging restored the moral order. Most commercial cop shows follow the same moral trajectory. For example, *Law and Order* is divided into two sections, and in each episode the depiction of a crime is followed by a trial of the accused. *Murder She Wrote* features at least a murder a week, yet how many of its prime-time audience (with an average age of 55) does Jessica Fletcher inspire to commit murder? Even the much criticized "woman in jeopardy" movie-of-the-week traditionally ends with the detection of the guilty party and the restoration of the moral order.

It would be impossible to impart moral lessons without depicting immorality. However, the amoral universe of the social engineer abhors depictions of aberrant behaviors. Since social science has no theology of free will, there is the assumption of a Pavlovian stimulus-response mechanism unmediated by moral choice. Therefore, any depiction of antisocial behavior is perceived as a threatening stimulus. Social science was given high status in the former Soviet Union, where dissidents were placed in mental hospitals, and conformity enforced with ruthless determination by secret police. Some parallel can be found in the politically correct "sensitivity training" now required on college campuses and in some workplaces.

Archetypes of the American Psyche

However, to a free and democratic republic such as the United States, the depiction of violence is not frightening in the least, since it reflects a fundamental confidence in individual freedom and personal liberty. Repeated illustrations of violence and immorality are necessary to impart ethical lessons to the citizenry just as "hellfire and brimstone" are used in sermons to emphasize the frightening prospect of hell. Likewise, acts of violence are often the means of resisting evil. Those who believe in "nonviolent conflict resolution" by highly paid "facilitators" have no use for a Clint Eastwood or a Ronald Reagan who says: "Make my day" and means it.

Antipathy towards television is nothing new in liberal American politics. It was Federal Communications Commission (FCC) Commissioner Newton Minow's railing against the vast wasteland" of TV Westerns in the Kennedy administration that led to the establishment of the Public Broadcasting Service, which currently allows us to watch high-class murders weekly on *Mystery!* and more than occasionally on *Masterpiece Theatre.* The cunning of history has proved Kennedy's FCC chairman wrong about the television environment he described so disdainfully. Westerns such as *Gunsmoke* now rightfully are recognized as classics,

58

archetypes of the American psyche.

The importance of Westerns as sources of moral instruction can be seen in the decision by the Family Channel (owned by Christian Coalition founder Pat Robertson) to syndicate *The Young Riders*. In 1991 the program was found to be the most violent on television, averaging 55 violent incidents per hour. The Family Channel found the series to be good family fare with a clear moral context and lack of gratuitous violence. As Robert Knight, director of cultural studies for the Family Research Council, noted in his analysis of *The Young Riders*:

> The moral factor is, indeed, crucial to measuring violence. Zeroing in solely on quantity eliminates the moral factor, on which it is far more difficult to find a consensus. The debate over TV violence is being conducted in a way similar to the gun-control issue. When the moral context is eliminated, the issue is framed entirely around the sheer number of guns, whether they belong to a hoodlum or to Joe Q. Law-Abiding Family Man. In the same way, all TV violence, whatever the moral context, is condemned by some as inherently wrong. On both issues, individual accountability is devalued, and the government stands to gain more control at the expense of individual freedom.

Don't Condemn the Good Guys

Knight's commonsense point stands in contradistinction to findings described as "not encouraging" by S. Robert Lichter and Stanley Rothman, who charged in their study that on prime-time television "acts of violence were committed by good guys more often than bad guys, and they were rarely condemned as illegal or morally wrong." Well, if acts of violence are being committed by good guys to stop bad guys, they should not be condemned. The policeman and the criminal are not morally equivalent actors. Lichter and Rothman complain that 278 good guys used violence compared with 212 bad guys and that "truth, justice, and the American way were defended by violence more often than they were threatened by it." One would hope so! There could be no better evidence than Lichter and Rothman's own data to indicate the moral universe of prime-time television is deeply conservative. . . .

Not a Government Issue

There can be no doubt that the explosion of cable networks and ensuing competition for viewership has led to a proliferation of tabloid programming, some of it extremely violent. In this respect the television universe today more closely represents the rest of the press, filled as it is with sensationalism.

Many rightfully find such material distasteful, and communities should always have the right to protect themselves against material that violates local standards. However, the answer to complaints about specific programs does not lie in intrusive actions by the federal government any more than the presence of violent and trashy novels or tabloid newspapers in supermarkets should require federal intervention. Calls for "v-chips" or other technological quick fixes completely miss the point, since morally uplifting programming based on Old Testament tales could be lumped into the same category as the most meretricious exploitation. The result, no doubt, could be the migration of violent programming to premium cable channels or direct broadcast satellite, which are not subject to FCC network content regulations. It might provide a powerful incentive for the telephone companies to deliver programming on a pay-per-view basis. Audiences would follow popular programming to their new venues.

Same Message

Since the early 1990s, a lot of films have come out that deal with the impact of gangs, drugs, and violence on city youth. The news media has criticized some of these movies—particularly *New Jack City* and *Juice*—for encouraging real-life violence. . . .

I disagree. Movies such as *Juice* attempt to realistically portray the problems faced by city youth. They don't promote violence. These movies show the downside of using or dealing drugs and joining gangs, and show that there are alternatives. . . .

It is because movies are dramatic, entertaining, and realistic that the audience will sit there for over an hour and watch them. Watching these films, you might even say to yourself, "These people [the filmmakers] really know what the deal is."

The basic message conveyed by *Juice* and *New Jack City* is similar to the one contained in lectures we get from our parents, the public service commercials we see on television, and the lessons we get in health class. Same message, different packaging. And the difference in the packaging will make young people more likely to listen and learn.

Daniel Jean-Baptiste, *New Youth Connections*, Special Reprint Edition, n.d.

Similarly, calls for "term limits" on station owners would be fruitless. In the early 1990s all the major networks changed hands, but the producers of programming remained the same. This is because audiences—more than owners—determine what programs are aired, as anyone familiar with commercial broadcasting understands. Tabloid programs were in fact dreamed up by syndicators locked out of the network marketplace, and then copied by ABC, NBC and CBS.

This is not to deny that there are real problems in American society, as William Bennett's *Index of Leading Cultural Indicators* has pointed out. And some viewers may resent the extent to which television has replaced sitting on the porch, playing cards or going to church. But let's not blame this shift in behavior on television violence. Television has been disruptive, because of its place in the home as an alternative source of cultural authority.

Further, much of the criticism of television violence comes from liberal social constructionists who believe that exposure to television violence makes people warlike. Such a naive pacifism is reminiscent of the view that if only GI Joe had not been for sale, the United States might never have remained in Vietnam.

Church—Not State

Instead of looking for easy answers, Americans concerned with the quality of television programming might follow the example of the Reverend Donald Wildmon and the American Family Association (AFA), who monitor shows for foul language, gratuitous violence and explicit sex. The group keeps detailed records and then brings pressure to bear on advertisers. The campaigns of the AFA and groups such as Terry Rakolta's Americans for Responsible Television (born out of disgust at *Married . . . With Children*) have been remarkably successful. The Reverend Calvin Butts of the Abyssinian Baptist Church in New York recently has had similar success in combating the pernicious influence of "gangsta" rap music in his Harlem community, and succeeded in removing the most offensive programming from the radio.

More churches would do well to follow suit and make media reform a priority. After all, it was pressure from the Roman Catholic church that spurred the Motion Picture Association of America to enforce the Motion Picture Code during what is now universally acknowledged as Hollywood's Golden Age. At the time, every script was examined for its moral implications and revised in consultation with the Motion Picture Association of America. In the early days of television, the National Association of Broadcasters enforced the Television Code with a parallel system. Similar pressure from religious circles today could have significant impact on cable television.

Moral uplift can come only from those with moral authority.

"Children from single-parent families are more prone to commit crime."

Single-Parent Families Cause Juvenile Crime

Robert L. Maginnis

Many Americans perceive a rise in violent crime among adolescents and link this to the growing number of single-parent families. In the following viewpoint, Robert L. Maginnis argues that such a link exists and that marriage and two-parent families are critical to crime prevention. Children from single-parent families, he argues, are more likely to have behavior problems because they tend to lack economic security and adequate time with parents. Boys who do not have fathers as male role models suffer especially, Maginnis adds. Maginnis is a policy analyst for the Family Research Council, a conservative research organization that represents those concerned with preserving the traditional family.

As you read, consider the following questions:

1. In James Q. Wilson's opinion, as quoted by Maginnis, what is the primary cause of crime?
2. Why, according to Maginnis, are children from single-parent homes more at risk for juvenile delinquency?
3. What two behaviors, according to the author, are unmarried men more prone to than married men?

From Robert L. Maginnis, "Crime and Its Roots: A Look Behind the Numbers," *Family Policy*, June 1994. Reprinted with permission.

Teens are increasingly the perpetrators—and the victims—of criminal behavior. The number of juveniles arrested under 18 years of age rose 17.4 percent from 1983 to 1992. Murder arrests among people under 18 years of age increased 128.1 percent; rape was up 24.7 percent; and aggravated assault was up 95.1 percent. . . .

The scope of the problem is illustrated by the growing number of young violent offenders. For example, between 1965 and 1992, the number of 12-year-olds arrested for violent crimes rose 211 percent; the number of 13- and 14-year-olds rose 301 percent; and the number of 15-year-olds rose 297 percent. . . .

Some of the violence among America's youth defies comprehension. In March 1994, CBS's *Eye on America* told a story about a violent teenager. At the dinner table on Halloween evening a few years ago, a 16-year-old boy was angered by his parents' refusal to allow him to go to a party. He left the table, loaded a shotgun and returned to the kitchen, killing his mother and stepfather.

Shocking incidents like this are all too common. In 1990, juvenile courts handled 1,264,800 serious crime cases, a 4 percent increase over 1989 and a 10 percent jump over 1986. The overall juvenile violent crime rate has risen 19 percent since 1989 and 41 percent since 1983. Arrests of juveniles under 18 years of age for violent crimes increased more than 57 percent between 1983 and 1992. During the same period, juvenile weapons violations jumped 117 percent.

Most worrisome is a trend summarized by Family Court Judge Richard Fitzgerald: "We are seeing juveniles committing more of the violent crimes at a younger age and with more destructive force and impact.". . .

The Roots of Crime

Blame for crime has been placed on poverty, genetic makeup, excess hormones, blood abnormalities, drug abuse, violence on television, a sick culture, bad parents and more.

A 1994 *Dallas Morning News* poll attributes crime to root causes that predominantly involve drugs and negligent parenting, but a majority also blame low morals, alcohol abuse, childhood academic problems and physical abuse.

James Q. Wilson, a UCLA political scientist, told CNN's *Moneyline*:

> [T]he root causes of crime are something that are typical of almost the entire globe. . . . It's not primarily the result of unemployment. It's not primarily the result of changes in the labor market. It reflects, in my view, a profound cultural shift that has overcome the western world during the last 30 years. To correct the bad consequences of that shift, we have to di-

rect our resources to very small children. . . . [I]f we can improve the way small children grow up by encouraging better parenting, by encouraging a better foster care system, by altering the welfare rules, we may have a chance of undoing some of the mischief that has been done by this cultural change.

The evidence suggests two of the primary roots of crime are the decline of the intact two-parent family and the breakdown of individual accountability.

Family Breakdown

Children from single-parent families are more prone to commit crime. This is because unmarried mothers often lack the skills to support a family or to manage a household effectively. Children from single-parent families are two to three times more likely to have emotional and behavioral problems than are children in two-parent families. They are more likely to drop out of high school, to get pregnant as teenagers, to abuse drugs, and to be in trouble with the law.

The *Journal of Research in Crime and Delinquency* reports that the most reliable indicator of violent crime in a community is the proportion of fatherless families. Fathers typically offer economic stability, a role model for boys, greater household security, and reduced stress for mothers. This is especially true for families with adolescent boys, the most crime-prone cohort.

When compared to children from two-parent families, children from single-parent homes are more prone to crime:

- They use drugs more heavily and commit more crimes throughout their lives.
- They are more likely to be gang members.
- They make up 70 percent of juvenile delinquents in state reform institutions.
- They account for 75 percent of adolescent murderers.
- They are 70 percent more likely to be expelled from school.

In addition, a 1991 research review published in the *Journal of Marriage and Family* found that growing up in a single-parent family is linked with increased levels of depression, stress, and aggression; a decrease in some indicators for physical health; higher incidence of needing the services of mental health professionals; and other emotional and behavioral problems.

Marriage: The Great Civilizer

Just as growing up in a married couple household reduces the likelihood that one will engage in criminal behavior, getting married also reduces criminal propensities. Throughout history, marriage has proved to be a great civilizer of the human male. It allows him to channel his innate hunter/predator instincts and energies into the role of provider/protector. It helps teach him responsibility and undermines his natural hedonism. Without the restraints of the marriage bond, men often abandon their children to seek pleasure. The impact on children's self-esteem and self-discipline is predictable.

Reprinted by permission of Mike Ramirez and Copley News Service.

David W. Murray, a Brandeis University anthropologist, notes that "the widespread failure to marry is a sign of impending disaster." He argues that marriage helps families multiply their economic capital by making kinsmen out of strangers. "A man with no relatives is a man with no concern for the shame or honor that his behavior might bring upon those he loves," Murray says. "He acts, therefore, without control or humanity."

Unmarried men are five times more likely to commit violent crimes than are married men. Although they represent a small minority of the male population over fourteen, they commit more than 80 percent of the violent crimes.

Breakdown of Individual Accountability

Former Los Angeles Police Department Assistant Chief Bob Vernon argues that many young people today have no moral compass to guide them. They have not been taught by parents and other adults to appreciate lifetime family commitment, submission to authority, loyalty, honesty and respect for others' property.

Unfortunately, parents today are devoting considerably less time to childrearing than did parents a generation ago. In fact, a 1991 study found that total parental time with children has dropped 40 percent since 1965. And Dr. Armand Nicholi of Harvard says that U.S. parents now spend less time with their children than parents in every other country in the world except Great Britain.

A lack of parent-child time has consequences. According to a 1993 Metropolitan Life Survey, "Violence in America's Public Schools," 71 percent of teachers and 90 percent of law enforcement officials state that the lack of parental supervision at home is a major factor contributing to the violence in schools. Students agree with this assessment to the tune of 61 percent for elementary and 76 percent for secondary children.

Vernon links this lack of individual accountability to the widespread cultural endorsement of hedonism. He argues that the seeking of pleasure as the chief good in life leads to a thriving illegal drug market and many other social ills. The pursuit of hedonism also spawns extramarital relationships, unbridled careerism, and the abandonment of family responsibility. Vernon states, "Many young people today lack a healthy sense of self-worth; they're angry and bitter. Life for them is grievous, a sour joke, something to dull with drugs and sex until it mercifully ends."

Deena Weinstein, a professor at DePaul University who teaches a sociology course on rock music, stated, "This generation's main attitude is irony. It's a generation that's already cynical about everything, including commercial success and fame and stardom.". . .

Americans perceive that crime is getting worse. This may seem out of line with crime statistics, but the changing face of crime has made citizens feel less safe. Contributing to this perception is the growing ineffectiveness of the criminal justice system, the growing number of young and violent criminals, and the rise in random crime. Strong law enforcement and pro-family changes in the culture appear to be the only way to reverse the trends of the national crime problem.

"Is there a positive relationship between the broken home and delinquency?" Apparently, no definite answer can be made."

Single-Parent Families May Not Cause Juvenile Crime

Kevin N. Wright and Karen E. Wright

Research has failed to clearly establish that single-parent families are a primary cause of juvenile delinquency, Kevin N. Wright and Karen E. Wright argue in the following viewpoint. Not only is data contradictory and inconclusive, the authors contend, but much of the research conducted during the 1950s and 1960s was flawed by bias against single mothers. Some studies, the authors maintain, indicate that the quality of family relationships is more significant than the absence of a parent in causing juvenile delinquency. Kevin N. Wright is a professor of criminal justice for the State University of New York's School of Education and Human Development. Karen E. Wright serves as the director of counseling services for the Planned Parenthood Association of Delaware and Otsego Counties in New York.

As you read, consider the following questions:

1. In the authors' opinion, why are the research results indicating a strong correlation between single-parent homes and juvenile delinquency inconclusive?
2. On what basis do the authors criticize the language commonly used to describe family arrangements?

From Kevin N. Wright and Karen E. Wright, *Family Life, Delinquency, and Crime: A Policymaker's Guide* (Washington, DC: Office of Juvenile Justice and Delinquency Prevention, May 1994), courtesy of the authors.

There is an intuitive appeal to the idea that a single parent, particularly when female, will be less able to effectively supervise, guide, and control a child or adolescent to insulate him or her from criminal or delinquent influences.

Research into the idea that single-parent homes may produce more delinquents dates back to the early nineteenth century. Officials at New York State's Auburn Penitentiary, in an attempt to discern the causes of crime, studied the biographies of incarcerated men. Reports to the legislature in 1829 and 1830 suggested that family disintegration resulting from the death, desertion, or divorce of parents led to undisciplined children who eventually became criminals.

Now, well over a century later, researchers continue to examine the family background of unique populations and reach similar conclusions. Like their forerunners, many current investigations lack control groups for comparisons but still offer some insight into what can happen to children in single-parent families. Ann Goetting, for example, found that only 30 percent of children arrested for homicide in Detroit between 1977 and 1984 lived with both parents. In a study of 240 women committed to the California Youth Authority in the 1960's, Jill Leslie Rosenbaum observed that only 7 percent came from intact families.

Conflicting Data

Two explanations of why single-parent families seem to produce more delinquents are frequently offered. Sociologists Ross L. Matsueda and Karen Heimer suggest that single parents can less effectively supervise their children simply because there is only one parent rather than two; consequently their children are more likely to come into contact with delinquent influences. Sanford G. Dornbusch and several of his colleagues offer a second explanation, specific to single mothers, suggesting that the mother gives the adolescent a greater say in what he or she can do, thus reducing control over the youth. However, the relationship between single parenthood and delinquency may not be as simple as these commonly held opinions imply.

Negley K. Teeters and John Otto Reinemann drew the following conclusion about the relationship in their 1950 textbook, *The Challenge of Delinquency:*

> For the student to wend his way through such a welter of conflicting opinion, coming as it does from experts, is indeed a confusing task. What he wants to know is: "Is there a positive relationship between the broken home and delinquency?" Apparently, no definite answer can be made to the question.

Thirty-six years and hundreds of studies later, L. Edward Wells and Joseph H. Rankin reached a similar conclusion: "Despite a sizable body of research extending across various academic disciplines, the question of the causal connections between broken homes and delinquency remains unresolved and ambiguous."

The literature reveals conflicting findings and opinions regarding the relationship between family structure and delinquency. The relationship is, indeed, complex. However, from the cumulative body of the research, consistent patterns emerge that provide useful information about the causal relationship.

Blaming the Victim

Dr. Alvin Poussaint, a noted Harvard psychiatrist, participated in a televised discussion of the tendency of American men toward violent behavior. Unfortunately, Dr. Poussaint argued that families, particularly mothers, are largely responsible for male violence. . . .

What a pathetic argument: our otherwise decent society has become the victim of its children because mothers have raised them poorly. . . .

What about a system which has produced a culture that glorifies and glamorizes violence in general and the violence of racism and male supremacy in particular?

Dr. Poussaint has done us a disservice by promoting an old theme that explains nothing and blames the victim.

Dee Myles, *People's Weekly World*, January 29, 1994.

Many studies examining the singular relationship between single-parent families and delinquency have found a positive relationship. Other studies have identified more specific breakdowns. For example, Robert D. Gove and Walter R. Crutchfield found the positive relationship to be true for males but not for females. Lawrence Rosen observed a positive association between single-parent households and delinquency for male children in black families. Deborah W. Denno discovered among black families that the positive association exists for males but not females. Robert L. Flewelling and Karl E. Bauman observed a positive relationship between single-parent families and the use of a controlled substance or engaging in sexual intercourse. C. Patrick Brady, James H. Bray, and Linda Zeeb, testing in a clinical setting, found that the children of single-parent families exhibited more behavioral problems. According to Laurence Steinberg, children from single-parent families also appear to be more susceptible to peer pressure. In an observation study of mother/child interaction, Carolyn Webster-Stratton found that single mothers issue more critical statements and that their children exhibit more deviant and noncompliant behaviors.

A major study of 1,517 boys by Rolf Loeber and several others explored the characteristics that linked with changes in offending over time. The researchers found that single parenthood correlated with delinquency across age groups from 7 to 8, 10 to 11, and 13 to 14. Children from single-parent homes were more likely to escalate their delinquency as they passed through adolescence, whereas children raised in two-parent homes were more likely to desist from delinquent behavior as they matured.

The National Incidence Studies on Missing, Abducted, Runaway, and Throwaway Children in America found that family division played a significant role in determining teenage runaways. "Thrownaway" children were more likely to come from single-parent homes. Furthermore, teenagers run away more often from families with stepparents and live-in boyfriends or girlfriends.

A Clouded Connection

Although the evidence is convincing, other studies contradict those cited. Rosen and Kathleen Neilson and M. Farnworth found no association between single-parent families and delinquency. Helene Raskin White, Robert J. Pandina, and Randy L. LaGrange found a positive relationship to heavy alcohol use but not to delinquency or drug abuse. Phyllis Gray-Ray and Melvin C. Ray identified no relationship between family type and delinquency for black children and adolescents. Additional support for this position was found by Naida M. Parson and James K. Mikawa, who observed no difference between the percentages of incarcerated and nonincarcerated blacks from broken homes.

The association between single-parent families and delinquency is further clouded by a series of studies claiming that negative effects of single parenthood may be caused by parental practices and family relations. In other words, the problems of single-parent families are explained by how parents relate to their children and how the family as a whole gets along. Several studies also suggest that the effect of single-parent homes is explained by conflict that occurred between the parents before and after the breakup.

Scott W. Henggeler suggested that greater autonomy for the adolescent, less parental supervision, less involvement with parents, and, consequently, increased susceptibility to peer pressure determine delinquency. These factors are more likely to be present in single-parent families, although not exclusively so. Along these same lines, Sadi Bayrakal and Teresa Kope claimed that children in single-parent families tend to grow up too fast. These children may have a greater expectation for independence from parental control. For blacks, the presence of a father in the adolescent's life appears to be important.

Other factors shown to influence this relationship are peer

70

pressure, personality, social class and criminality on the part of the father, and conflict and coping strategies. Birgitte R. Mednick and her colleagues indicated that divorce followed by a stable family constellation is not associated with increased risk, but divorce followed by additional changes in family configuration significantly increases risk, particularly for adolescent males.

A Better Predictor

Three literature reviews help us to disentangle these disparate research findings. Loeber and Magda Stouthamer-Loeber reviewed 15 studies, including 40 analyses of structural relationships. The review encompassed information indicating that 33 of the 40 assessments (83 percent) were statistically significant and that the effect of marital separation appeared to be somewhat greater on younger children. Marital discord was shown to be a better predictor of delinquency than family structure. Two studies found that the death of a parent did not have the same effect as divorce on the child's behavior, which suggests that it is family relations, not just separation, that affects delinquency. Loeber and Stouthamer-Loeber reviewed two studies of supervision that speak to the single-parent/delinquency question. Stouthamer-Loeber and her fellow researchers found that single mothers and unhappily married mothers supervised less diligently and that more of them had negative opinions of their children. H.S. Goldstein found that high supervision in father-absent families reduced the probability of arrest.

A meta-analysis of 50 studies by Wells and Rankin suggests that the effect of broken homes on delinquency is real and consistent, but of relatively low magnitude. The "prevalence of delinquency in broken homes is 10 to 15 percent higher than in intact homes." The effect is strongest for minor offenses and weakest for serious offenses. The Wells and Rankin review indicates that the type of breakup—death, desertion, or divorce—affects delinquency determination. Further, there appears to be no appreciable or consistent difference in effect on boys versus girls or blacks versus whites, no consistent effect related to the child's age, and, finally, no consistent effect of stepparents' presence within the family.

The general patterns observed by Loeber and Stouthamer-Loeber and Wells and Rankin regarding family structure and delinquency are similarly described by Sara McLanahan and Karen Booth, who discuss more general consequences of growing up in mother-only families. During the 1950's and 1960's, researchers viewed divorce and births to unmarried mothers as pathological, and they expected children in such situations to exhibit undesirable behaviors. In the 1970's, that view began to change. Researchers argued that the differences between mother-only and two-parent families could be explained by other factors such as poverty. Now, studies examining the cumulative findings of the research are recognizing certain negative consequences of growing up in single-parent homes. While these recent studies acknowledge that there may be nothing inherently pathological with single parenthood, such a structure may lead to a set of conditions that contribute to delinquency, for example, greater autonomy for the adolescent, less parental control, and increased susceptibility to peer pressure. Therefore, designing programs that assist the single parent in supervising the child and that free the parent to spend more time with the child may reduce delinquency.

"Broken" Is Not Necessarily Bad

Up until now, this report, like most others, has been somewhat cavalier in its use of language describing different structural arrangements of families, not stopping to precisely define what is being studied. Many researchers use the words "broken" and "intact" to describe family structures. These words are value-laden. The word "broken" possesses a negative connotation and inasmuch as the purpose of this research is to determine the effect of family structure, it seems inappropriate to use a negative label for single parenthood. Consider at least two examples when the loss of a parent may strengthen family relations: (1) The death of a parent, though tragic for the family, may draw members together, bonding them in a manner that gives the surviving parent considerable influence over the children. (2) The loss of a violent or psychologically abusive parent may remove the source that is pushing children out of the family and creating individual stress. One study found that the outcome of parental absence depended on the competence of the remaining parent. In fact, "separation seemed to have little or no adverse effect when the alternative was an intact family with conflict, low parental esteem, paternal alcoholism, or criminality." A more precise definition of family structure is needed than a simple distinction between one- and two-parent families.

As Wells and Rankin have pointed out, one must contend with conceptual and measurement issues when contemplating and attempting to understand the relationship of single-parent homes to delinquency. Conceptual elements that must be considered include factors about the parent, parent absence, and the entire household. Regarding the parent, we must consider whether the parent is the biological, step-, or adoptive parent. Perhaps the "parent" is a guardian, for example, the grandparents, foster parents, or some other significant and caring adult. Issues of absence must be viewed in terms of frequency and duration, amount of contact (total or partial), visitation, shared custody, and neglect. And we must include a close examination of the conceptual elements of the household. The middle-class, nuclear family living in a single-family home is only one form of family. Many others exist and produce positive outcomes for their children. It is important to look at who lives in the house or apartment. This may vary considerably and is an important cultural and socioeconomic factor that is virtually unexplored. Thinking about and understanding these concepts will help to clarify any inquiry into family structure and delinquency.

Social Status Plays a Key Role

McLanahan and Booth presented three explanations for the relationship between single-parent or mother-only families and delinquency: (1) economic deprivation, (2) socialization, and (3) neighborhood. In this viewpoint, a fourth theory is added: the justice system's response.

Looking first at economic deprivation, Denno and David P. Farrington, in their longitudinal research, showed delinquency to be related to the mother's income at the time of the child's birth and to the father's irregular employment. Other studies indicate that one of two single mothers lives in poverty compared with one in ten two-parent families with children. Additionally, studies have found single mothers to have fewer resources (e.g., time and money) to invest in their children.

The second theory, socialization, includes factors that can attenuate the effect of single parenthood, such as autonomy, supervision, affection, and conflict. To this list Merry Morash and Lila Rucker add "low hopes for education." Single parents may be less able to properly supervise, monitor, guide, and support their children to ensure their conformity to societal rules.

The third theory, neighborhood, recognizes that many single-parent families live in social isolation and in economically deprived neighborhoods. This demographic reality results in decreased opportunity for economic mobility and is associated with greater likelihood that children will quit school or become pregnant as teenagers.

Marcus Felson and Lawrence E. Cohen stated that two-parent households provide increased supervision and surveillance of property, while single parenthood increases likelihood of delinquency and victimization simply by the fact that there is one less person to supervise adolescent behavior. Robert J. Sampson confirmed this second hypothesis and suggested that single parenthood indirectly decreases formal control because there is evidence of less participation in community and schools by single-parent families. Judith Blau and Peter Blau argued that marital disruption is a proxy for overall disorganization and alienation in the community.

73

Fourth, and finally, the criminal justice system may respond differently to the children from single-parent rather than two-parent families. Richard E. Johnson argued that family structure is not related to frequency or seriousness of self-reported illegal behavior but is related to self-reported trouble with police, school, and juvenile court. Johnson concluded that officials may be more likely to respond to the behavior of children from mother-only families. Cogent to this point, John Hagan and Alberto Palloni found in their study of the intergenerational transmission of crime within families that after controlling for child-rearing practices, evidence suggested that labeling of family members by crime-control agents tended to reproduce criminal behavior.

In summary, what do we know about single parenthood's contribution to delinquency?

- Economic conditions inherent to single-parent families may place children at greater risk.
- Socialization of children residing in single-parent homes may differ from those residing with two parents.
- "Bad" neighborhoods, where single parents often reside, may contribute to delinquency.
- The ways in which the system or officials from formal institutions such as school, police, and courts respond to children from single-parent homes may result in these children being more likely to be identified as delinquent.

What remains unknown or unclear?

- We lack a good understanding of parental practices and differences among the various types of households.
- We tend to see single-parent families in a monolithic way, neglecting attempts to understand the variations among these families that may produce successes as well as failures. Heidi L. Hartman indicated that at least 25 percent of all families with children are single-parent households. Most of these families do not produce delinquent children.
- Similarly, we lack knowledge about the variation among two-parent families.

74

"Biological factors ranging from inherited personality traits and genetic defects to biochemical imbalances and brain damage . . . can skew the odds a child will become violent."

Biological Factors Contribute to Juvenile Crime and Violence

Nancy Wartik

Studies indicate that biological factors, including genetics, may predispose a child to commit violent crimes, Nancy Wartik argues in the following viewpoint. Additional physiological risk factors, she maintains, can result from brain damage or physical harm that occurs during fetal development or early childhood. According to Wartik, this data proves that while environment does play a role, biological factors are significant determinants of whether a child will become a violent criminal. Wartik is a contributing editor for *American Health* magazine.

As you read, consider the following questions:

1. What idea does Wartik use *The Bad Seed* and *The Good Son* to illustrate?
2. How do antisocial, crime-prone children differ physiologically from their peers, according to Wartik?
3. According to Adrian Raine, as quoted by Wartik, what factor can counteract biological risk factors that predispose children to violent criminal behavior?

Nancy Wartik, "Why Some Kids Go Wrong," *McCall's*, April 1994. Reprinted by permission.

On a humid August morning in 1993, in the quiet New York town of Savona, Eric Smith, age 13, intercepted four-year-old Derrick Robie on his way to a park recreation program and offered to show him a shortcut. Hesitatingly, Derrick set off with Eric. He never made it to the park. That same day the little boy's savagely beaten body was discovered outside the park. A week later Eric confessed the crime to police and was charged with second-degree murder. . . .

Sadly, this tragedy is not an isolated one. Jon Venables and Robert Thompson of Liverpool, England, made international headlines in November 1994 when they were convicted of murdering James Bulger, age two. The two boys, ten years old at the time of the slaying, lured James away from his mother in a shopping mall, took him to a nearby railroad track, beat him brutally and left him to be cut in half by a train.

Also in 1993 three young sisters from California's San Fernando Valley were found guilty of the stabbing death of a 62-year-old neighbor. A librarian, she had befriended the sisters, who were then ages 12, 15 and 16. And less than four months after Derrick Robie's death, a 15-year-old boy from the same town shot his brother dead in a quarrel over a bottle of cold medicine, leaving Savona residents to ask what was happening to their children.

Born to Be Evil?

What would drive youngsters to commit such heinous crimes? Are they born to be evil—bad seeds, like the murderous brats played by Patty McCormack in 1956's *The Bad Seed* and Macaulay Culkin in 1993's *The Good Son*? Or is it something in their upbringing that has warped their moral sense or robbed them of the ability to resolve conflicts peaceably?

The question of what makes a child turn to extreme violence grows more urgent as juvenile-crime rates soar. Between 1988 and 1992, according to the National Center for Juvenile Justice, the number of arrests for violent crime among those under age 18 rose 47 percent. These statistics refer not to unruly adolescents who are shoplifting or delinquent but to youngsters who are killing, maiming and raping. In that same time the number of arrests for murder in the same age group rose 51 percent.

There are no simple answers to the enigma of whether some children are born bad. Research indicates that biological factors ranging from inherited personality traits and genetic defects to biochemical imbalances and brain damage suffered in the womb can skew the odds a child will become violent. Yet experts argue that no one is predestined to a life of crime; they contend that influences like repeated abuse, extreme neglect, poverty, media violence and easy access to guns play the major role in molding kids into criminals. As the debate simmers, a growing body of evidence suggests the truth lies somewhere in between.

How Heredity Can Stack the Deck

Serial murderer Jeffrey Dahmer had just turned 18 when he slew his first victim. In his memoir, *A Father's Story*, Lionel Dahmer ponders whether there were hereditary reasons his son went so terribly astray. He discusses tendencies in himself that he recognizes, hideously magnified, in his son, and describes Jeffrey's mother as psychiatrically disturbed. "I . . . wonder," he writes, "if [the] potential for great evil . . . resides deep in the blood that some of us fathers and mothers may pass on to our children at birth."

Scientists have spent years searching for a "crime gene." In the 1970s there was much interest in the discovery that men with an extra X or an extra Y chromosome were found at higher rates among the prison population. But further research discredited the idea that such men were born criminals. Instead, their chromosomal pattern apparently produced traits like lower IQ, which seems to predispose people to criminality. Today most scientists search not for genes that dictate behavior but for physiological risk factors that increase the potential of someone being violence-prone.

A Biological Link to Antisocial Behavior

Many neuroscientists now believe that one key factor in violent behavior is a failure of impulse control. In at least a subset of violent offenders, the inability to control certain drives and desires may lead to acts of violence and aggression. No one believes that a simple neurochemical produces antisocial behavior, but evidence from several laboratories indicates that the neurotransmitter serotonin is a key player in impulse control.

Nancy Touchette, *Journal of NIH Research*, February 1994.

Heredity can, however, stack the deck toward violence through its influence on personality and temperament, which are linked to physiological factors. Antisocial, aggressive children tend to fit a certain profile: They are fearless, impulsive risk takers who are restless, have a low attention span and trouble empathizing with others and want immediate gratification of their needs. Some of these characteristics may have genetic influences, notes David Kosson, a psychologist at the University of North Carolina at Greensboro who studies antisocial disorders.

Such children even seem to differ physiologically from their

77

well-behaved peers. Among other things, they have lowered heart rates and slower brain-wave activity. Criminal behavior in this group, explains University of Southern California psychologist Adrian Raine, an expert in the physiology of violence, may actually be an attempt to achieve normal levels of physiological stimulation.

This need for extra stimulation might help explain a known pattern of fire setting, cruelty to animals and property destruction among seriously violent youngsters. Lending support to this idea is a 1988 study of serial killers, which found that as children more than a third exhibited such destructive behavior. Jeffrey Dahmer, for example, used to nail animals to trees.

Body Chemistry Gone Astray

Scientists are also exploring the role of certain neurochemicals—particularly serotonin, a brain transmitter that regulates mood and emotion—in triggering violence. The latest research has linked serotonin imbalances to impulsive acts of aggression.

In a 1992 study, Markus J.P. Kruesi, M.D., chief of child and adolescent psychiatry at the University of Illinois Institute for Juvenile Research, found that in a group of adolescents with disruptive behavior, concentrations of serotonin in the spinal fluid were the best predictor of the severity of physical aggression.

Both high and low levels of the neurochemical norepinephrine, which regulates the body's fight-or-flight response in threatening situations, have been associated with overaggressive tendencies: Too much may predispose someone to explosive rages; too little, to acts of premeditated, cold-blooded cruelty.

Evidence suggests that sometimes imbalances of these brain chemicals can be genetic. Dutch and American researchers who studied several generations of aggression-prone men from a Dutch family discovered the men had a defect in a gene that helps regulate levels of serotonin and norepinephrine. (Women can be carriers of the gene, which sits on the X chromosome, but aren't affected, because with two X chromosomes to a man's one, a woman still has a backup that's normal.)

The Time Bomb of Brain Damage

Another factor that can increase the risk of juvenile violence is damage to a developing brain. In a 1994 study, the University of Southern California's Raine reviewed medical records of 9,000 women who gave birth several years earlier. He found that birth complications, such as a breech birth, significantly raised the likelihood that the child would have a violent criminal record by age 18—although he notes that upbringing is also key in molding these children.

Raine speculates the infants may have experienced damage to

a part of the brain that helps curb aggressive impulses. Or there could have been general impairment of the brain's information-processing abilities, making it harder for a child to comprehend societal rules or to function well in school.

In a 1988 study of 13 young murderers—11 boys and two girls, ages 13 to 17—New York University School of Medicine child psychiatrist Dorothy Otnow Lewis, M.D., found more than 50 percent had signs of major brain dysfunction resulting from falls, accidents or other traumas. In a comparison group of non-violent delinquents, only 6 percent showed signs of impairment. A mother's use of recreational drugs, alcohol or tobacco during pregnancy has also been linked to her child's risk of future criminality, again because these substances may harm a fetal brain.

In a 1990 exploration of the roots of criminality, law professor Deborah Denno of Fordham University in New York City found a dramatic connection between lead poisoning, which can impair brain function, and juvenile crime. Denno looked at a variety of factors in children's backgrounds, including their medical records. She found that discipline problems in school were the strongest predictor of an arrest record from ages seven to 22—and that lead poisoning was the strongest predictor of school discipline problems.

Finally, the male hormone testosterone, which helps shape brain development while a child is in the womb and affects brain function throughout life, has been linked to violent behavior. Sociologist Lee Ellis of Minot State University in North Dakota believes testosterone accounts for the fact that 90 percent of violent criminals of any age are men. He notes that higher levels of testosterone in the brain may spur the kind of stimulation-seeking behavior associated with violent criminality.

Learning to Kill

Still, many experts don't buy the notion that biology alone creates children who kill. "Violence is learned behavior," insists University of Michigan psychologist Leonard Eron, who recently chaired the American Psychological Association's Commission on Violence and Youth. "You can have birth complications or genetic tendencies, but you don't act a certain way unless that's how you've learned to behave."

Being abused as a child or witnessing domestic battering is the most-often-cited environmental factor in juvenile violence. Indeed, New York University's Lewis found young murderers were nearly twice as likely as ordinary delinquents to have been physically abused and six times as likely to have seen violence in the home. "Newspapers reporting stories of juvenile murderers often say, 'It was a wonderful family—this was just a wicked kid,'" she says. "But scratch the surface and you'll usually find a lot has happened to that child that no one realizes."

Psychologist Charles Patrick Ewing of Buffalo, author of the 1990 book *Kids Who Kill*, agrees that most violent children have been severely maltreated or neglected: "It's the single most consistent finding in juvenile-homicide cases. If you're brutalized and given the message you're worthless, what will stop you from killing? You'll have no respect for your own life, no respect for the lives of others. The idea of the sanctity of life won't deter you."

Robert Thompson, one of the Liverpool murderers, had a father who abandoned him and a mother who spent much of her time at the local pub. Eric Smith was reportedly raised with a family member who has an explosive temper. The California sisters grew up with ongoing domestic violence, according to newspaper accounts. And serial killers almost invariably come from abusive families, says former FBI agent Robert K. Ressler, who has interviewed dozens of these murderers.

"The concept of someone coming out of a good home and suddenly going crazy isn't reality," he says. "It's their background that produces these abnormal people." Lionel Dahmer admits Jeffrey's childhood was one of utter neglect. Ted Bundy, the notorious serial killer executed in 1989, never knew his real father and spent the first three years of his life with a grandfather who was described as extremely violent.

But what of children from seemingly nurturing homes who nonetheless commit atrocious crimes? In July 1992 Shannon Garrison, her sister, Melissa, and Melissa's boyfriend, Alan Gould, ages 15 to 17, were charged with the premeditated stabbing death of the girls' mother one night as she slept. Shannon and Alan pleaded guilty to murder; after two hung-jury trials, Melissa's case is to be retried.

A divorced social worker, Betty Garrison, age 45, was described as a caring parent by her Gulfport, Mississippi, community. The only motive offered for the killing, says police detective Danny Holloway, who took the teens' statements, was "that the mother grounded the girls a lot and wouldn't let them talk to friends on the phone." But, he adds, "they didn't seem to have been disciplined any different than my parents disciplined me—and I didn't kill my mama."

Which Kids Turn Violent—and Why

In a society where young children watch an average of 25 hours of television per week—with five violent acts an hour during prime time and 26 an hour on Saturday morning—some experts say media influences are a major force in fostering aggression. "When four- and five-year-old kids watch these programs over and over, they start to believe that aggression is appropriate, that everyone acts this way," says University of Michigan psychologist Eron. "They think that's how you get things you don't have, or that's how you relieve frustration."

The judge in the James Bulger case noted that violent films may have planted the seed of the murder. The manner of James's death resembled a scene in the horror movie *Child's Play 3*, which Venables's father had rented not long before the murder. (Police, however, stress that there's no evidence that either boy had seen the film.)

But such theories of juvenile aggression can't explain why the majority of children who are exposed to media violence or are abused don't explode under pressure. "Most children who come from disadvantaged backgrounds don't commit crimes," points out Stanton Samenow, an Alexandria, Virginia, psychologist specializing in criminal behavior. "Nearly every juvenile offender I've talked with has had brothers or sisters who suffered similar hardships and didn't turn to crime. Why is that?"

Many researchers are coming to believe that biology and environment must interact to turn a child bad. "I've almost never seen a case where either neurological problems or abuse alone accounted for murder by a child," says New York University child psychiatrist Lewis. "It's the abuse plus the underlying physiological vulnerability."

In his study of mothers who'd had difficult deliveries, University of Southern California psychologist Raine found their offspring were at increased risk of crime only if they had also been rejected or severely neglected by their mother. "Birth complications predisposed the children to violence, but there had to be a trigger in the environment as well," he says. "When children were brought up supportively, it counteracted the biological damage."

Similarly, the researchers who studied the Dutch family with the genetic defect say inheriting the problem gene didn't invariably cause hostile behavior in the family members. "It may make someone more vulnerable to aggressive impulses, but this defect doesn't doom him to be violent," says Xandra O. Breakefield, a neuroscientist at Massachusetts General Hospital in Charlestown who worked on the study. "There are many ways to compensate for it."

Breaking the Spell of Violence

Such findings, in one sense, provide a measure of hope: Biology alone need not seal a child's fate. Yet in a society where so many pregnant women abuse drugs or alcohol, where child abuse is epidemic, where there's easy access to guns and where images of violence are pervasive, biology and environment are conspiring to send children down the wrong path. And when a child has traveled down this path too far, it can be hard to redeem him or her. "It's sad," says Yale University child psychologist Alan Kazdin, "but right now we know much better how to make children aggressive and violent than how to make them stop."

That makes prevention critical, say experts, who call for the targeting of issues such as handgun control, media violence, child abuse and even the presence of lead-based paint in homes. Some schools have implemented intervention programs to teach children how they can use nonviolent tactics in problem-solving situations.

At the individual level it's crucial that parents or other adults in a child's life intervene quickly if they spot troubling behavior patterns. In his book *Before It's Too Late: Why Some Kids Get Into Trouble and What Parents Can Do About It*, Samenow shows how an incorrigible ten-year-old, Rory, was reformed.

"Rory shoplifted, pilfered from classmates and did poorly in school though he was bright," he explains. "He fantasized about raping young girls . . . and his parents complained that his behavior was controlling their home life." Samenow helped the boy analyze specific thought patterns causing his destructive behavior. He counseled his parents to set stricter limits, insisting that Rory show he could be trusted before he was given more freedom and that he face consequences when he misbehaved.

Though Rory's parents remained skeptical throughout two years of counseling, Samenow recently received a letter from the boy's mother saying her son was graduating from high school and contemplating a career in law enforcement.

One wonders what might have been had someone stepped in to rescue Eric Smith. Derrick Robie might still be alive—and Eric not facing the possibility of life behind bars.

"Most violent behavior is learned behavior."

Environmental Factors Contribute to Juvenile Crime and Violence

Delbert S. Elliott

Experts have long debated whether violent behavior results from biological factors (such as a genetic predisposition to violence) or from environmental factors (such as poverty and racial discrimination). In the following viewpoint, Delbert S. Elliott describes various environmental factors that he says contribute to juvenile crime and violence. According to Elliott, these detrimental influences include violent and permissive families, unstable neighborhoods, and delinquent peer groups. Elliott is the director of the Institute of Behavioral Science's Center for the Study and Prevention of Violence at the University of Colorado in Boulder.

As you read, consider the following questions:

1. According to the author, under what circumstances does violent behavior become rational?
2. What is the "critical feature" of crime-prone neighborhoods, according to Elliott?
3. In the author's assessment, what are the two major effects of growing up in poor, minority families and disorganized neighborhoods?

From Delbert S. Elliott, "Youth Violence: An Overview," working paper, Center for the Study of Youth Policy, University of Pennsylvania, Philadelphia, 1993. Reprinted by permission of the author.

Across America, people are afraid. This fear is not restricted to those living in the most disadvantaged neighborhoods in our large cities, but extends to residents of affluent suburban communities, and even small towns and rural areas. For many, the violence signals a general breakdown in the social order. There seem to be no safe places; the violence extends into our homes, neighborhoods, schools, daycare facilities, shopping malls, and workplaces. The perpetrators are often relatives, friends or acquaintances of the victim. So much of the violence seems petty, senseless, or random, suggesting a wanton disregard for human life. And both perpetrators and victims are increasingly our adolescents and children. . . .

Learned Behavior

Most violent behavior is learned behavior. We all have some potential for violent behavior; we have observed others using violence and know how to do it. But while it may be a part of nearly everyone's behavioral repertoire, most persons have non-violent ways of achieving their purposes which are effective in most situations. Further, their commitment to conventional norms and values inhibits their use of violent behavior, and they are embedded in social networks (family and friends) and situations where this type of behavior would have serious negative ramifications. Under these circumstances, violent behavior becomes irrational.

Unfortunately, for too many youth, violence is either the only or the most effective way to achieve status, respect, and other basic social and personal needs. There is little prosocial modeling of alternative ways of dealing with conflict. Like money and knowledge, violence is a form of power, and for some youth, it is the only form of power available. When such limited alternatives are combined with a weak commitment to moral norms (internal controls) and little monitoring or supervision of behavior (external controls), violent behavior becomes rational. The potential rewards are great, the perceived costs minimal.

The Family

The initial causes of violence are found in the early learning experiences in the family. They involve 1) weak family bonding and ineffective monitoring and supervision; 2) exposure to and reinforcement for violence in the home; and 3) the acquisition of expectations, attitudes, beliefs, and emotional responses which support or tolerate the use of violence.

Early exposure to violence in the family may involve witnessing either violence or physical abuse. Research suggests that these forms of exposure to violence during childhood increase the risk of violent behavior during adolescence by as much as

84

40%. Still, most youth who are victims of physical abuse do not go on to become serious violent offenders. While exposure to real violence and physical abuse on the part of family members has stronger modeling effects, heavy exposure to violence on television is also causally linked to later violence. In many homes, television is the *de facto* babysitter, with little or no monitoring or supervision of content. When there is strong family bonding, effective teaching of moral values and norms, and effective monitoring of behavior, the effect of exposure to violence on T.V. is probably negligible; without this protection, its effect can be quite strong. What is learned is not only how to do violence, but a desensitization to violence and rationalizations for disengaging one's moral obligations to others.

A Recipe for Violence

Without jobs, people in the inner cities live impoverished, overcrowded lives. Without steady incomes, the people in poor neighborhoods cannot support businesses, and thereby jobs, in their area. The only "business opportunities" are either drugs or prostitution. . . .

With the drugs comes the war among the dealers for market share. The fight among the drug dealers and the theft that the jobless addicts resort to to finance their habit frighten urbanites into buying handguns "for protection." These guns are then often stolen or are taken to school by the gun owners' children to show off to their friends. Either way, the guns end up on the streets, in the hands of young people who are at an age where proving your "manhood" in front of your peers is all-important. It is a guaranteed recipe for violence.

Erik Parsels, *New Unionist*, March 1994.

Even if violence is not modeled in the home, research suggests that the absence of effective social bonds and controls, together with a failure of parents to teach (and children to internalize) conventional norms and values, puts children at risk of later violence. In fact, parental neglect may have an even stronger effect than physical abuse on later violence, as it appears to be more damaging to the subsequent course of youth development and involves three times as many youth.

There is also evidence that certain individual temperaments and acquired biological deficits may complicate or interfere with parents' efforts to develop good internal controls in their children. Antisocial personality and attention deficit disorders, a fearless and impulsive temperament, exposure to lead and other neurotoxins, and serious head injuries, for example, may make it difficult for even the best parents to develop strong family bonding and good internal controls and provide effective monitoring of their children.

Families with a high risk for child abuse are those with parents or caretakers who have limited problem-solving skills, poor impulse control and a history of violent behavior during adolescence. These caretakers are frequently young, low-income, single-parent, minority women with four or more children in the household. Fathers, when present, tend to be part-time employed and have a limited education. These families have few resources and are experiencing both social isolation and economic stress. They have few alternatives and limited social supports from extended family or friendship networks which might provide social controls on their behavior and non-violent alternatives for managing their children.

The Neighborhood

Some neighborhoods also provide opportunities for learning and engaging in violence. The presence of gangs and illegal markets, particularly drug distribution networks, not only provide high levels of exposure to violence, but violent role models, and positive rewards for serious violent activity. Single-parent families, ineffective parenting, violent schools, high dropout rates, high adolescent pregnancy rates, substance abuse, and high unemployment rates are all concentrated in such neighborhoods.

While these neighborhoods are areas with high concentration of poverty, their critical feature that is most directly related to the high rates of violence, crime, and substance use, is the absence of any effective social or cultural organization. High levels of transiency make it difficult to establish common values and norms, informal support networks, and effective social controls. High chronic unemployment results in social isolation from legitimate labor markets, and undermines the relevance of completing school. Illegitimate enterprises and gangs emerge, in part because the neighborhood has no effective means of resisting such activity, and in part as a means of providing some stable social organization for youth and some economy for the neighborhood. Not all poor neighborhoods are disorganized, however, and those that are effectively organized have low rates of violent behavior, crime, and substance use. Poverty is linked to violence through disorganized neighborhoods.

The effect of living in such neighborhoods can devastate the family's attempt to provide a healthy, conventional upbringing for their children. Not only are there few social reinforcements for conventional lifestyles to support this type of parenting, but conventional opportunities are limited by racism, discrimination,

86

social isolation from the labor market, and few resources. There are often greater opportunities for participation in gangs and the illicit economy, which offer relatively quick and substantial rewards that seem to offset the risks associated with violence. One effect of participation in these types of activities is that youth are at high risk for becoming victims as well as perpetrators of violence; a second is that such youth frequently abandon the pursuit of more conventional goals, drop out of school, get pregnant, and become enmeshed in health-compromising and dysfunctional lifestyles that arrest the normal course of adolescent development. Such youth are ill-prepared to enter conventional adult roles.

The School

While patterns of behavior learned in early childhood (e.g., aggressiveness) carry over into the school context, the school has its own potential for generating conflict, frustration, and violent responses to these situations. A successful non-violent social adjustment at home increases the likelihood but does not *guarantee* a successful non-violent adjustment to school and peers. These are new social systems which have to be negotiated, where one must find her or his own niche. They each have their own performance demands and developmental tasks to complete. Failure to meet these school and peer performance expectations (e.g., academic success, peer approval, personal competence and independence, self-efficacy, and a capacity for developing and maintaining interpersonal relationships and intimacy) creates stress and conflict. The combination of new conflicts and reduced levels of monitoring and supervision in these contexts increases the likelihood that violence will emerge in response to these problems.

During junior and senior high school, a clear adolescent status hierarchy emerges, and much of the violence at school is related to competition for status and status-related confrontations. Ability tracking also contributes to a collective adaptation to school failure and peer rejection by grouping academically poor students and aggressive troublemakers together in the same classes. Delinquent peer groups tend to emerge from these classes, and individual feelings of anger, rejection, and alienation are mutually reinforced in these groups. The strongest and most immediate cause of the actual onset of serious violent behavior is involvement with a delinquent peer group. Here is where violence is modeled, encouraged, and rewarded, and where justifications for disengaging one's moral obligation to others are taught and reinforced. The effects of early exposure to violence, weak internal and family controls, and aggressive behavior patterns developed in childhood all influence the type of friends one chooses,

87

and the type of friends, in turn, largely determines what behavior patterns will be modeled, established, and reinforced during adolescence. However, a strong bond to parents is a protective factor which insulates youth from the influence of delinquent friends as long as the friendship network is not dominated by such youth.

Gangs are a subtype of adolescent peer group, with a more formal identity and membership requirements. They tend to involve more homogeneously delinquent youth, often actively recruiting persons for their fighting skills or street smarts. In some instances, membership entails violent behavior as an initiation ritual. However, not all gangs are involved in serious violent behavior or drug distribution. They often serve some positive functions, particularly in disorganized neighborhoods. They not only provide youth a sense of acceptance, belonging, and personal worth (which most friendships do), but also a safe place to stay, food, clothing, and protection from abusive parents. But like delinquent groups more generally, joining a gang greatly increases the risk of serious violence, both perpetration and victimization. Likewise, leaving a gang or delinquent peer group substantially reduces the risk of serious violence.

Drugs and Guns

The relationship between substance use and violence is complicated. Alcohol is implicated in over half of all homicides and of assaults in the home. Parents who abuse alcohol (and illicit drugs) are more prone to be physically abusive to and neglectful of their children. But while problem drinkers are more likely to have a history of violent behavior, they are not disproportionately represented among violent offenders as compared with non-violent offenders. Pharmacological studies find no simple dose-response relationship between alcohol use and violent behavior. While alcohol is clearly implicated in violent behavior, the exact mechanism has not yet been established.

In general, the use of psychoactive drugs has not been linked pharmacologically to violent behavior. The effect of marijuana and opiate drugs actually appears to inhibit violence, although withdrawal may precipitate an increased risk of violence. There is some evidence that drug addicts commit violent crimes to support their drug habit, but this appears to be a relatively rare phenomenon. The clearest drug-violence connection is for selling drugs; the drug distribution network is extremely violent.

Between 1985 and 1993 the firearm-related homicide rate for adolescents has increased over 150%, and firearms now account for nearly three-fourths of all homicides of young black men. Surveys estimate that 270,000 guns are taken to school each day. It is not clear whether the increase in gun-related violence is simply the result of greater gun availability. However, violent events involving guns are 3 to 5 times more likely to result in death than those involving knives, the next most lethal weapon.

Not much is known about why today's youth, in increasing numbers, are carrying guns. Anecdotal evidence suggests it is to "show off," to ensure "respect" and acquiescence from others, or for self-defense. In part, it appears to be a response to the perception that public authorities cannot protect youth or maintain order in their neighborhoods or at school. There is evidence that dropouts, drug dealers, and those with a prior record of violent behavior are more likely to own a gun than are other adolescents. And the vast majority (80%) of firearms used in crimes are obtained by theft or some other illegal means.

Transition to Adulthood

The successful transition into adult roles (i.e., work, marriage, parenting) appears to reduce involvement in violent behavior. In one national study, nearly 80% of adolescents who were serious violent offenders reported no serious violent offenses during their adult years (to age 30). However, nearly twice as many black as white youth continued their offending after age 21. Among those employed at age 21, rates of continuity were low, and there were no differences in rates of continuity by race.

Race and class differences in serious violent offending are small during adolescence, but become substantial during the early adult years. This difference does not appear to be the result of differences in predisposition to violence, but in the continuity of violence once initiated. Race, in particular, is related to finding and holding a job, and to marriage and stable-cohabitating rates. In essence, race and poverty are related to the successful transition from adolescent to adult roles.

It appears that growing up in poor, minority families and disorganized neighborhoods has two major effects directly related to violent behavior. First, when it comes time to make the transition into adulthood, there are limited opportunities for employment which, in turn, reduces the chances of marriage. Employment and marriage are two primary definers of adult status. Secondly, there is evidence that growing up in poor, disorganized neighborhoods inhibits the normal course of adolescent development. Youth from these neighborhoods have lower levels of personal competence, self-efficacy, social skills, and self-discipline. Many are not adequately prepared to enter the labor market even if jobs were available. They are, in some ways, trapped in an extended adolescence and continue to engage in adolescent behavior.

"The number of guns continues to grow along with the numbers of youth who have become all too willing to use them."

Guns Contribute to Juvenile Crime and Violence

The Educational Fund To End Handgun Violence

The Educational Fund To End Handgun Violence is a Washington, D.C., research and advocacy organization dedicated to ending violence caused by the use of firearms. In the following viewpoint, the fund argues that the widespread availability of handguns in America has contributed to the escalating number of murders committed by juveniles in recent years. According to the fund, the accessibility of handguns combined with young people's inability to fully comprehend the consequences of their actions frequently results in violent and tragic consequences.

As you read, consider the following questions:

1. By what percentage did the number of fifteen-year-old males charged with murder increase between 1985 and 1990, according to the authors?
2. What is the leading cause of death for black males between the ages of fifteen and nineteen, as reported by the fund?
3. What points does the fund illustrate with the stories of Jamel and Andre?

From *Kids and Guns: A National Disgrace*, 3rd ed. (Washington, DC: Educational Fund To End Handgun Violence, 1993). Copyright 1993 by The Educational Fund To End Handgun Violence. Reprinted with permission.

An epidemic of youth violence is sweeping the streets of our nation's cities, both large and small, and has begun to infiltrate suburban and rural areas where residents previously believed themselves immune from the carnage.

A Northeastern University study entitled "Recent Trends in Violent Crimes: A Closer Look" indicates that the increased rate of criminal homicide in every city or town with a population of over 25,000 people is due to the increased number of homicides committed by youth.

In many cities and towns, political, community and business leaders are only now beginning to understand the enormity of the problem and have only recently begun to consider solutions. Meanwhile, the number of guns continues to grow along with the numbers of youth who have become all too willing to use them.

Not only are more children being shot to death, but more are doing the shooting. From 1985 to 1990 the number of teenagers murdered by firearms doubled; at the same time the number of 15-year-old males charged with murder increased by 217%.

If action is not taken soon to rescue the children trapped in this ever increasing cycle of violence, then the United States is at risk of losing an entire generation. The victims will not only be those who were killed, but also the survivors, scarred by growing up in virtual war zones.

Every day 13 children under the age of 19 are killed by gunfire and scores more are injured. Why is this happening and how long will the country let it continue? . . .

The Availability of Firearms

The homicide death rate among young people is rising as is the rate of youth charged with homicide. Historically, the rate of homicide has always been higher for males than females and much higher for black males than white males—so much higher that every year since 1969 the leading cause of death for black males 15 through 19 years of age has been firearm homicide. Sixty percent of deaths for black males 15–19 years old are direct results of firearm injury, while 23% of deaths for white males 15–19 years old directly result from firearm injury. These numbers illustrate the huge difference between black male and white male firearm death rates. However, even among white males, firearms are responsible for an alarmingly high number of deaths.

At the heart of these problems is the far too easy accessibility of firearms. By federal law, anyone under the age of 21 is not allowed to buy a handgun and anyone under the age of 18 is not allowed to buy a long gun, but these statutes do not prevent young people from obtaining firearms. Older friends, unknowing parents, and illegal street sales are sources from which a firearm can be obtained easily. The availability of firearms has made firearm injuries the second leading cause of death behind motor vehicle accidents for youth ages 10–19. For black males ages 10–19, the rate of death from firearms now exceeds that from motor vehicle accidents.

The vast majority of homicides are committed with a firearm. In 1990, 91% of black male homicides for the ages 15–19 involved a firearm, while 77% of white male homicides for the same ages involved a firearm. Guns make it easy to kill, far easier than any other weapon commonly available. The easy availability of handguns is greatly responsible for the skyrocketing murder rate in this country.

Arrest Rates for Criminal Homicide per 100,000 Males Within Selected Age Groups

Age Groups	1985	1990	1991	% Change 1985–1991
12 and under	0.1	0.1	0.2	100%
13–14	4.0	8.8	9.6	140%
15	11.8	31.0	37.4	217%
16	22.4	56.5	57.7	158%
17	34.5	72.4	76.1	121%

Glenn Pierce and James Fox, "Recent Trends in Violent Crimes: A Closer Look," October 1992.

A common stereotype that the public holds is of a masked intruder killing and robbing at whim, but, in fact, nearly half of the homicides in America today involve people who know one another. Friends, family members, and acquaintances are much more likely to commit a homicide than is someone unknown to the victim. According to the FBI's Uniform Crime Report, only 15% of homicide victims were murdered by strangers in 1991; in an additional 39% of murders the relationship was unknown. A plurality of murders occurs between friends and family members.

"Trigger-Happy"

Young people in particular tend to be very rash and have little sense of the consequences of their actions. James Fox, one of the authors of the Northeastern University report, points out the difference between a 45-year-old with a gun and a 14-year-old with a gun: "A 45-year-old with a gun in his hand, although he may be a better shot, is not as likely to use that gun as a 14-year-old. Fourteen-year-olds tend to be trigger-happy. . . . They'll pull that trigger if someone looks at them the wrong way. They'll pull that trigger if someone swears at them. They'll pull that trigger without thinking about the consequences." As violence has become commonplace in our society, more and more young people have come to see gun violence as an acceptable way to solve problems. For them, there is nothing unusual about a handful of children being shot in a weekend. There is nothing extraordinary about a child being shot in school. The pervasiveness of gun violence in our society and the passive permissiveness shown by our society towards gun violence has not only made our streets unsafe, but helped mold a generation of children who think gun violence is as American as baseball and apple pie. The rampant exposure of youth to weapons of such deadly force has resulted in the tragic waste of too many young lives.

James Fox explains some of the reasons for the increase in violence:

> Clearly we have become a more violent society. The recent wave of youth violence cannot be explained away as a function of demographic shifts or changes in criminal justice policy. Compared with their parents when they were teenagers, the new youth generation has more dangerous drugs in their bodies, more deadly weapons in their hands and are being socialized into a culture having a far more casual attitude toward violence.

A Deadly Combination

The deadly combination of guns and the rashness of youth is increasingly common and there are many chilling examples. A *New York Times* article examined the reasons young men cite for using a gun. Although most people would consider resorting to a gun only in life-threatening situations, to these young men it seemed like an appropriate response in less-threatening situations. (The young men in the article were all serving life sentences.)

• Jamel, a 13-year-old boy, was upset about being ignored by girls. After running into a hallway where a crack dealer had been watching Jamel's latest run-in with girls who had ignored him, Jamel decided to get even. "I was going to ask him for the gun," Jamel said, "but he just gave it to me. He said, 'Yo, go rob 'em.'" Jamel and another boy chased the girls, only to find the girls mocking Jamel again. With that, Jamel fired the gun, killing one of the girls.

• Andre, a 15-year-old boy, was scared of being beaten up by a group of boys in his neighborhood. He already had been assaulted by the boys before, when he finally decided not to be intimidated any longer. When he saw the boys next, he did not avoid them, choosing to face them with a gun. One of the boys jumped up to confront Andre. "I had the gun behind my back, but he could see it," Andre said. "I'm telling him to back away or else I'm going to have to shoot. I was petrified I was going to get jumped. The guy said, 'If you shoot me, you better kill me, because I'll get you.'" Andre got him first. "I didn't intend to kill him," Andre said later, "I just wanted to scare him. I didn't know it would go off so easily."

Needless Destruction

These two accounts illuminate the needless destruction that regularly occurs on our streets. Neither boy realized the consequences of his actions. They were unable to equate pulling the trigger of a gun with someone falling to the street dead. They did not understand the dangers of weapons, and did not give much thought to what might happen to them or their victims after they pulled the trigger. What they did see was a quick, easy solution to a problem. Their responses to these scenarios are considered appropriate by many other youth and adults. Violent retaliation to threats or slights both real and imagined has become all too common and accepted.

Reflecting the current violent trends, the firearm homicide rate for black males 15 through 19 years of age nearly tripled to 105.3 deaths per 100,000 during the years 1985 to 1990. During this same time period, the firearm homicide rate for white males and black females 15–19 years of age doubled, increasing to 9.7 and 10.4 per 100,000 respectively. Still, black males are nearly 11 times more likely to be murdered with a firearm than their white counterparts. To put this in perspective, one should consider that if the rest of the population was being murdered by firearms at a rate equal to that of young black males, over 260,000 Americans would be shot to death each year. It is troubling that more is not being done by community and national leaders to curb the firearm homicide rate of young black males.

According to the FBI Uniform Crime Report published in 1992, 80% of firearm homicides are committed with a handgun, although inadequacies in the reporting system probably understate the number of handgun homicides. Handguns show up as murder weapons because they are extremely easy to conceal and extremely lethal. As for youth, kids increasingly bring their guns to school, carry them around their neighborhoods and use them to settle disputes.

It is easy to reduce this epidemic to cold facts and figures, forgetting about the families and loved ones left behind to deal with their losses. Gun violence ended the lives of nearly 5,000 young people in 1990. They never had a chance to realize their potential. Families and friends are left to struggle with their death and feelings of loss. More and more Americans have devastating stories to tell about how gun violence has shaped their lives.

8

8
VIEWPOINT

"Simply living in [an inner-city] environment places young people at special risk of falling victim to aggressive behavior."

Inner-City Culture Contributes to Juvenile Crime and Violence

Elijah Anderson

In the following viewpoint, Elijah Anderson argues that the culture of inner-city black communities encourages and reinforces aggressive behavior among juveniles. According to Anderson, life in the inner cities is regulated by a "code of the streets," which legitimizes the use of violence as a means of gaining respect from one's peers. Anderson is the Charles and William Day Professor of the Social Sciences at the University of Pennsylvania and the author of *Streetwise: Race, Class, and Change in an Urban Community.*

As you read, consider the following questions:

1. How must inner-city teenagers present themselves in order to conform to the code of the streets, according to the author?
2. In what ways can nerve be displayed, according to Anderson?
3. What does the author say is the source of most disputes between teenage girls?

From Elijah Anderson, "The Code of the Streets" from *The Code of the Streets*. Excerpted from the article originally in *The Atlantic Monthly* 273, no. 5 (May 1994): 81-94. Copyright © 1994 by Elijah Anderson. Reprinted with the permission of the author and W.W. Norton & Company, Inc.

Of all the problems besetting the poor inner-city black community, none is more pressing than that of interpersonal violence and aggression. It wreaks havoc daily with the lives of community residents and increasingly spills over into downtown and residential middle-class areas. Muggings, burglaries, carjackings, and drug-related shootings, all of which may leave their victims or innocent bystanders dead, are now common enough to concern all urban and many suburban residents. The inclination to violence springs from the circumstances of life among the ghetto poor—the lack of jobs that pay a living wage, the stigma of race, the fallout from rampant drug use and drug trafficking, and the resulting alienation and lack of hope for the future.

Simply living in such an environment places young people at special risk of falling victim to aggressive behavior. Although there are often forces in the community which can counteract the negative influences, by far the most powerful being a strong, loving, "decent" (as inner-city residents put it) family committed to middle-class values, the despair is pervasive enough to have spawned an oppositional culture, that of "the streets," whose norms are often consciously opposed to those of mainstream society. These two orientations—decent and street—socially organize the community, and their coexistence has important consequences for residents, particularly children growing up in the inner city. Above all, this environment means that even youngsters whose home lives reflect mainstream values—and the majority of homes in the community do—must be able to handle themselves in a street-oriented environment.

A Code of the Streets

This is because the street culture has evolved what may be called a code of the streets, which amounts to a set of informal rules governing interpersonal public behavior, including violence. The rules prescribe both a proper comportment and a proper way to respond if challenged. They regulate the use of violence and so allow those who are inclined to aggression to precipitate violent encounters in an approved way. The rules have been established and are enforced mainly by the street-oriented, but on the streets the distinction between street and decent is often irrelevant; everybody knows that if the rules are violated, there are penalties. Knowledge of the code is thus largely defensive; it is literally necessary for operating in public. Therefore, even though families with a decency orientation are usually opposed to the values of the code, they often reluctantly encourage their children's familiarity with it to enable them to negotiate the inner-city environment.

At the heart of the code is the issue of respect—loosely defined as being treated "right," or granted the deference one deserves.

96

However, in the troublesome public environment of the inner city, as people increasingly feel buffeted by forces beyond their control, what one deserves in the way of respect becomes more and more problematic and uncertain. This in turn further opens the issue of respect to sometimes intense interpersonal negotiation. In the street culture, especially among young people, respect is viewed as almost an external entity that is hard-won but easily lost, and so must constantly be guarded. The rules of the code in fact provide a framework for negotiating respect. The person whose very appearance—including his clothing, demeanor, and way of moving—deters transgressions feels that he possesses, and may be considered by others to possess, a measure of respect. With the right amount of respect, for instance, he can avoid "being bothered" in public. If he is bothered, not only may he be in physical danger but he has been disgraced or "dissed" (disrespected). Many of the forms that dissing can take might seem petty to middle-class people (maintaining eye contact for too long, for example), but to those invested in the street code, these actions become serious indications of the other person's intentions. Consequently, such people become very sensitive to advances and slights, which could well serve as warnings of imminent physical confrontation. . . .

Although almost everyone in poor inner-city neighborhoods is struggling financially and therefore feels a certain distance from the rest of America, the decent and the street family in a real sense represent two poles of value orientation, two contrasting conceptual categories. The labels "decent" and "street," which the residents themselves use, amount to evaluative judgments that confer status on local residents. The labeling is often the result of a social contest among individuals and families of the neighborhood. Individuals of the two orientations often coexist in the same extended family. Decent residents judge themselves to be so while judging others to be of the street, and street individuals often present themselves as decent, drawing distinctions between themselves and other people. In addition, there is quite a bit of circumstantial behavior—that is, one person may at different times exhibit both decent and street orientations, depending on the circumstances. Although these designations result from so much social jockeying, there do exist concrete features that define each conceptual category.

Decent Families

Generally, so-called decent families tend to accept mainstream values more fully and attempt to instill them in their children. Whether married couples with children or single-parent (usually female) households, they are generally "working poor" and so tend to be better off financially than their street-oriented neighbors. They value hard work and self-reliance and are willing to sacrifice for their children. Because they have a certain amount of faith in mainstream society, they harbor hopes for a better future for their children, if not for themselves. Many of them go to church and take a strong interest in their children's schooling. Rather than dwelling on the real hardships and inequities facing them, many such decent people, particularly the increasing number of grandmothers raising grandchildren, see their difficult situation as a test from God and derive great support from their faith and from the church community.

"Sure Enoughs of the Street"

Marcus Tramble remembers when he was in grade school and his family moved to the South Side, Chicago, housing project where he lives now, a 16-story building with what Marcus calls "cages" of wire mesh on the balconies. New to the neighborhood, he had to prove himself regularly, in fistfights and shouting matches.

Now he fits in and has earned a measure of respect. . . .

Much of what Marcus knows about the streets he learned by watching older men, men who now are either dead or in jail. "I learned from their mistakes," he said.

Those lessons are what he calls "the sure enoughs of the street":

• "Never, ever, steal from somebody, especially if they're rollin'," which means selling drugs.

• "Never, ever, mess with another brother's woman."

• "Never, ever, hit someone's mother."

• "And never, ever, disrespect somebody."

"Respect," he said, "is like money: you got to have it. No respect, no cooperation; no cooperation, no money."

Don Terry, *New York Times*, April 13, 1993.

Extremely aware of the problematic and often dangerous environment in which they reside, decent parents tend to be strict in their child-rearing practices, encouraging children to respect authority and walk a straight moral line. They have an almost obsessive concern about trouble of any kind and remind their children to be on the lookout for people and situations that might lead to it. At the same time, they are themselves polite and considerate of others, and teach their children to be the same way.

At home, at work, and in church, they strive hard to maintain a positive mental attitude and a spirit of cooperation.

Street Parents

So-called street parents, in contrast, often show a lack of consideration for other people and have a rather superficial sense of family and community. Though they may love their children, many of them are unable to cope with the physical and emotional demands of parenthood, and find it difficult to reconcile their needs with those of their children. These families, who are more fully invested in the code of the streets than the decent people are, may aggressively socialize their children into it in a normative way. They believe in the code and judge themselves and others according to its values.

In fact the overwhelming majority of families in the inner-city community try to approximate the decent-family model, but there are many others who clearly represent the worst fears of the decent family. Not only are their financial resources extremely limited, but what little they have may easily be misused. The lives of the street-oriented are often marked by disorganization. In the most desperate circumstances people frequently have a limited understanding of priorities and consequences, and so frustrations mount over bills, food, and, at times, drink, cigarettes, and drugs. Some tend toward self-destructive behavior; many street-oriented women are crack-addicted ("on the pipe"), alcoholic, or involved in complicated relationships with men who abuse them. In addition, the seeming intractability of their situation, caused in large part by the lack of well-paying jobs and the persistence of racial discrimination, has engendered deep-seated bitterness and anger in many of the most desperate and poorest blacks, especially young people. The need both to exercise a measure of control and to lash out at somebody is often reflected in the adults' relations with their children. At the least, the frustrations of persistent poverty shorten the fuse in such people—contributing to a lack of patience with anyone, child or adult, who irritates them.

In these circumstances a woman—or a man, although men are less consistently present in children's lives—can be quite aggressive with children, yelling at and striking them for the least little infraction of the rules she has set down. Often little if any serious explanation follows the verbal and physical punishment. This response teaches children a particular lesson. They learn that to solve any kind of interpersonal problem one must quickly resort to hitting or other violent behavior. Actual peace and quiet, and also the appearance of calm, respectful children conveyed to her neighbors and friends, are often what the young mother most desires, but at times she will be very aggressive in

99

trying to get them. Thus she may be quick to beat her children, especially if they defy her law, not because she hates them but because this is the way she knows to control them. In fact, many street-oriented women love their children dearly. Many mothers in the community subscribe to the notion that there is a "devil in the boy" that must be beaten out of him or that socially "fast girls need to be whupped." Thus much of what borders on child abuse in the view of social authorities is acceptable parental punishment in the view of these mothers.

Sporadic Mothers

Many street-oriented women are sporadic mothers whose children learn to fend for themselves when necessary, foraging for food and money any way they can get it. The children are sometimes employed by drug dealers or become addicted themselves. These children of the street, growing up with little supervision, are said to "come up hard." They often learn to fight at an early age, sometimes using short-tempered adults around them as role models. The street-oriented home may be fraught with anger, verbal disputes, physical aggression, and even mayhem. The children observe these goings-on, learning the lesson that might makes right. They quickly learn to hit those who cross them, and the dog-eat-dog mentality prevails. In order to survive, to protect oneself, it is necessary to marshal inner resources and be ready to deal with adversity in a hands-on way. In these circumstances physical prowess takes on great significance.

In some of the most desperate cases, a street-oriented mother may simply leave her young children alone and unattended while she goes out. The most irresponsible women can be found at local bars and crack houses, getting high and socializing with other adults. Sometimes a troubled woman will leave very young children alone for days at a time. Reports of crack addicts abandoning their children have become common in drug-infested inner-city communities. Neighbors or relatives discover the abandoned children, often hungry and distraught over the absence of their mother. After repeated absences, a friend or relative, particularly a grandmother, will often step in to care for the young children, sometimes petitioning the authorities to send her, as guardian of the children, the mother's welfare check, if the mother gets one. By this time, however, the children may well have learned the first lesson of the streets: survival itself, let alone respect, cannot be taken for granted; you have to fight for your place in the world.

Campaigning for Respect

These realities of inner-city life are largely absorbed on the streets. At an early age, often even before they start school, children from street-oriented homes gravitate to the streets, where they "hang"—socialize with their peers. Children from these generally permissive homes have a great deal of latitude and are allowed to "rip and run" up and down the street. They often come home from school, put their books down, and go right back out the door. On school nights eight- and nine-year-olds remain out until nine or ten o'clock (and teenagers typically come in whenever they want to). On the streets they play in groups that often become the source of their primary social bonds. Children from decent homes tend to be more carefully supervised and are thus likely to have curfews and to be taught how to stay out of trouble.

When decent and street kids come together, a kind of social shuffle occurs in which children have a chance to go either way. Tension builds as a child comes to realize that he must choose an orientation. The kind of home he comes from influences but does not determine the way he will ultimately turn out—although it is unlikely that a child from a thoroughly street-oriented family will easily absorb decent values on the streets. Youths who emerge from street-oriented families but develop a decency orientation almost always learn those values in another setting—in school, in a youth group, in church. Often it is the result of their involvement with a caring "old head" (adult role model).

In the street, through their play, children pour their individual life experiences into a common knowledge pool, affirming, confirming, and elaborating on what they have observed in the home and matching their skills against those of others. And they learn to fight. Even small children test one another, pushing and shoving, and are ready to hit other children over circumstances not to their liking. In turn, they are readily hit by other children, and the child who is toughest prevails. Thus the violent resolution of disputes, the hitting and cursing, gains social reinforcement. The child in effect is initiated into a system that is really a way of campaigning for respect.

Might Makes Right

In addition, younger children witness the disputes of older children, which are often resolved through cursing and abusive talk, if not aggression or outright violence. They see that one child succumbs to the greater physical and mental abilities of the other. They are also alert and attentive witnesses to the verbal and physical fights of adults, after which they compare notes and share their interpretations of the event. In almost every case the victor is the person who physically won the altercation, and this person often enjoys the esteem and respect of onlookers. These experiences reinforce the lessons the children have learned at home: might makes right, and toughness is a virtue, while humility is not. In effect they learn the social meaning of fighting. When it is left virtually unchallenged, this understanding becomes an ever more important part of the child's working conception of the world. Over time the code of the streets becomes refined.

Those street-oriented adults with whom children come in contact—including mothers, fathers, brothers, sisters, boyfriends, cousins, neighbors, and friends—help them along in forming this understanding by verbalizing the messages they are getting through experience: "Watch your back." "Protect yourself." "Don't punk out." "If somebody messes with you, you got to pay them back." "If someone disses you, you got to straighten them out." Many parents actually impose sanctions if a child is not sufficiently aggressive. For example, if a child loses a fight and comes home upset, the parent might respond, "Don't you come in here crying that somebody beat you up; you better get back out there and whup his ass. I didn't raise no punks! Get back out there and whup his ass. If you don't whup his ass, I'll whup your ass when you come home." Thus the child obtains reinforcement for being tough and showing nerve.

While fighting, some children cry as though they are doing something they are ambivalent about. The fight may be against their wishes, yet they may feel constrained to fight or face the consequences—not just from peers but also from caretakers or parents, who may administer another beating if they back down. Some adults recall receiving such lessons from their own parents and justify repeating them to their children as a way to toughen them up. Looking capable of taking care of oneself as a form of self-defense is a dominant theme among both street-oriented and decent adults who worry about the safety of their children. There is thus at times a convergence in their child-rearing practices, although the rationales behind them may differ.

Self-Image

By the time they are teenagers, most youths have either internalized the code of the streets or at least learned the need to comport themselves in accordance with its rules, which chiefly have to do with interpersonal communication. The code revolves around the presentation of self. Its basic requirement is the display of a certain predisposition to violence. Accordingly, one's bearing must send the unmistakable if sometimes subtle message to "the next person" in public that one is capable of violence and mayhem when the situation requires it, that one can take care of oneself. The nature of this communication is largely determined by the demands of the circumstances but can include facial expressions, gait, and verbal expressions—all of which are geared mainly to deterring aggression. Physical ap-

102

pearance, including clothes, jewelry, and grooming, also plays an important part in how a person is viewed; to be respected, it is important to have the right look.

Even so, there are no guarantees against challenges, because there are always people around looking for a fight to increase their share of respect—or "juice," as it is sometimes called on the street. Moreover, if a person is assaulted, it is important, not only in the eyes of his opponent but also in the eyes of his "running buddies," for him to avenge himself. Otherwise he risks being "tried" (challenged) or "moved on" by any number of others. To maintain his honor he must show he is not someone to be "messed with" or "dissed." In general, the person must "keep himself straight" by managing his position of respect among others; this involves in part his self-image, which is shaped by what he thinks others are thinking of him in relation to his peers.

Objects play an important and complicated role in establishing self-image. Jackets, sneakers, gold jewelry, reflect not just a person's taste, which tends to be tightly regulated among adolescents of all social classes, but also a willingness to possess things that may require defending. A boy wearing a fashionable, expensive jacket, for example, is vulnerable to attack by another who covets the jacket and either cannot afford to buy one or wants the added satisfaction of depriving someone else of his. However, if the boy forgoes the desirable jacket and wears one that isn't "hip," he runs the risk of being teased and possibly even assaulted as an unworthy person. To be allowed to hang with certain prestigious crowds, a boy must wear a different set of expensive clothes—sneakers and athletic suit—every day. Not to be able to do so might make him appear socially deficient. The youth comes to covet such items—especially when he sees easy prey wearing them. . . .

Respect and Violence

Many inner-city young men in particular crave respect to such a degree that they will risk their lives to attain and maintain it. The issue of respect is thus closely tied to whether a person has an inclination to be violent, even as a victim. In the wider society people may not feel required to retaliate physically after an attack, even though they are aware that they have been degraded or taken advantage of. They may feel a great need to defend themselves *during* an attack, or to behave in such a way as to deter aggression (middle-class people certainly can and do become victims of street-oriented youths), but they are much more likely than street-oriented people to feel that they can walk away from a possible altercation with their self-esteem intact. Some people may even have the strength of character to flee, without any thought that their self-respect or esteem will be diminished.

In impoverished inner-city black communities, however, particularly among young males and perhaps increasingly among females, such flight would be extremely difficult. To run away would likely leave one's self-esteem in tatters. Hence people often feel constrained not only to stand up and at least attempt to resist during an assault but also to "pay back"—to seek revenge—after a successful assault on their person. This may include going to get a weapon or even getting relatives involved. Their very identity and self-respect, their honor, is often intricately tied up with the way they perform on the streets during and after such encounters. This outlook reflects the circumscribed opportunities of the inner-city poor. Generally people outside the ghetto have other ways of gaining status and regard, and thus do not feel so dependent on such physical displays.

Manhood

On the street, among males these concerns about things and identity have come to be expressed in the concept of "manhood." Manhood in the inner city means taking the prerogatives of men with respect to strangers, other men, and women—being distinguished as a man. It implies physicality and a certain ruthlessness. Regard and respect are associated with this concept in large part because of its practical application: if others have little or no regard for a person's manhood, his very life and those of his loved ones could be in jeopardy. . . .

Central to the issue of manhood is the widespread belief that one of the most effective ways of gaining respect is to manifest "nerve." Nerve is shown when one takes another person's possessions (the more valuable the better), "messes with" someone's woman, throws the first punch, "gets in someone's face," or pulls a trigger. Its proper display helps on the spot to check others who would violate one's person and also helps to build a reputation that works to prevent future challenges. But since such a show of nerve is a forceful expression of disrespect toward the person on the receiving end, the victim may be greatly offended and seek to retaliate with equal or greater force. A display of nerve, therefore, can easily provoke a life-threatening response, and the background knowledge of that possibility has often been incorporated into the concept of nerve.

True nerve exposes a lack of fear of dying. Many feel that it is acceptable to risk dying over the principle of respect. In fact, among the hard-core street-oriented, the clear risk of violent death may be preferable to being "dissed" by another. The youths who have internalized this attitude and convincingly display it in their public bearing are among the most threatening people of all, for it is commonly assumed that they fear no man. As the people of the community say, "They are the baddest dudes on the street." They often lead an existential life that may acquire meaning only when they are faced with the possibility of imminent death. Not to be afraid to die is by implication to have few compunctions about taking another's life. Not to be afraid to die is the quid pro quo of being able to take somebody else's life—for the right reasons, if the situation demands it. When others believe this is one's position, it gives one a real sense of power on the streets. Such credibility is what many inner-city youths strive to achieve, whether they are decent or street-oriented, both because of its practical defensive value and because of the positive way it makes them feel about themselves. The difference between the decent and the street-oriented youth is often that the decent youth makes a conscious decision to appear tough and manly; in another setting—with teachers, say, or at his part-time job—he can be polite and deferential. The street-oriented youth, on the other hand, has made the concept of manhood a part of his very identity; he has difficulty manipulating it—it often controls him.

Conflict Among Girls

Increasingly, teenage girls are mimicking the boys and trying to have their own version of "manhood." Their goal is the same —to get respect, to be recognized as capable of setting or maintaining a certain standard. They try to achieve this end in the ways that have been established by the boys, including posturing, abusive language, and the use of violence to resolve disputes, but the issues for the girls are different. Although conflicts over turf and status exist among the girls, the majority of disputes seem rooted in assessments of beauty (which girl in a group is "the cutest"), competition over boyfriends, and attempts to regulate other people's knowledge of and opinions about a girl's behavior or that of someone close to her, especially her mother.

A major cause of conflicts among girls is "he say, she say." This practice begins in the early school years and continues through high school. It occurs when "people," particularly girls, talk about others, thus putting their "business in the streets." Usually one girl will say something negative about another in the group, most often behind the person's back. The remark will then get back to the person talked about. She may retaliate or her friends may feel required to "take up for" her. In essence this is a form of group gossiping in which individuals are negatively assessed and evaluated. As with much gossip, the things said may or may not be true, but the point is that such imputations can cast aspersions on a person's good name. The accused is required to defend herself against the slander, which can result in arguments and fights, often over little of real substance. Here again is the problem of low self-esteem, which encourages

105

youngsters to be highly sensitive to slights and to be vulnerable to feeling easily "dissed." To avenge the dissing, a fight is usually necessary.

Because boys are believed to control violence, girls tend to defer to them in situations of conflict. Often if a girl is attacked or feels slighted, she will get a brother, uncle, or cousin to do her fighting for her. Increasingly, however, girls are doing their own fighting and are even asking their male relatives to teach them how to fight. Some girls form groups that attack other girls or take things from them. A hard-core segment of inner-city girls inclined toward violence seems to be developing. As one thirteen-year-old girl in a detention center for youths who have committed violent acts told me, "To get people to leave you alone, you gotta fight. Talking don't always get you out of stuff." One major difference between girls and boys: girls rarely use guns. Their fights are therefore not life-or-death struggles. Girls are not often willing to put their lives on the line for "manhood." The ultimate form of respect on the male-dominated inner-city street is thus reserved for men.

A Limited View

In the most fearsome youths such a cavalier attitude toward death grows out of a very limited view of life. Many are uncertain about how long they are going to live and believe they could die violently at any time. They accept this fate; they live on the edge. Their manner conveys the message that nothing intimidates them; whatever turn the encounter takes, they maintain their attack—rather like a pit bull, whose spirit many such boys admire. The demonstration of such tenacity "shows heart" and earns their respect.

This fearlessness has implications for law enforcement. Many street-oriented boys are much more concerned about the threat of "justice" at the hands of a peer than at the hands of the police. Moreover, many feel not only that they have little to lose by going to prison but that they have something to gain. The toughening-up one experiences in prison can actually enhance one's reputation on the streets. Hence the system loses influence over the hard core who are without jobs, with little perceptible stake in the system. If mainstream society has done nothing *for* them, they counter by making sure it can do nothing *to* them.

106

"Kids of whatever race, creed, or color are most likely to become criminally depraved when they are morally deprived."

A Lack of Moral Guidance Causes Juvenile Crime and Violence

John J. DiIulio Jr.

In the following viewpoint, John J. DiIulio Jr. argues that moral poverty—an absence of concerned adults capable of teaching children right from wrong—is responsible for the rising number and increasing seriousness of crimes committed by juveniles. According to DiIulio, moral poverty produces violent young criminals who are indifferent to the suffering of their victims. DiIulio is a professor of politics and public affairs at Princeton University and the director of the Center for Public Management at the Brookings Institution, a public policy research organization.

As you read, consider the following questions:

1. According to Mark S. Fleisher, cited by the author, what types of homes do juvenile street criminals come from?
2. What two developmental defects drive the behavior of juvenile "super-predators," in DiIulio's view?
3. What two reasons does the author give to support his contention that religion is the solution to juvenile crime?

John J. DiIulio Jr., "The Coming of the Super-Predators," *Weekly Standard*, November 27, 1995. Reprinted by permission of the author.

Lynne Abraham doesn't scare easily. Abraham is the no-nonsense Democratic district attorney of Philadelphia. The city's late tough-cop mayor, Frank Rizzo, baptized her "one tough cookie." The label stuck, and rightly so. Abraham has sent more mafiosi to prison than Martin Scorcese, stood up (all 5'2" of her) to violent drug kingpins, won bipartisan support in this Congress for wresting control of the city's jail system from an ACLU-brand federal judge, and publicly shamed the know-nothing literati who want to free convicted cop-killer Mumia Abu-Jamal. Today various of her colleagues at the non-partisan National District Attorneys Association describe her as "suite smart and street smart," "a genuine law-and-order liberal," and "probably the best big-city D.A. in the country."

Big Trouble

All true. So pay attention, because Lynne Abraham is scared.

In a recent interview, Abraham used such phrases as "totally out of control" and "never seen anything like it" to describe the rash of youth crime and violence that has begun to sweep over the City of Brotherly Love and other big cities. We're not just talking about teenagers, she stressed. We're talking about boys whose voices have yet to change. We're talking about elementary school youngsters who pack guns instead of lunches. We're talking about kids who have absolutely no respect for human life and no sense of the future. In short, we're talking big trouble that hasn't yet begun to crest.

And make no mistake. While the trouble will be greatest in black inner-city neighborhoods, other places are also certain to have burgeoning youth-crime problems that will spill over into up-scale central-city districts, inner-ring suburbs, and even the rural heartland. To underscore this point, Abraham recounted a recent town-hall meeting in a white working-class section of the city that has fallen on hard times: "They're becoming afraid of their own children. There were some big beefy guys there, too. And they're asking me what am *I* going to do to control *their* children."

I interviewed Abraham, just as I have interviewed other justice-system officials and prison inmates, as a reality check on the incredibly frightening picture that emerges from recent academic research on youth crime and violence. All of the research indicates that Americans are sitting atop a demographic crime bomb. And all of those who are closest to the problem hear the bomb ticking.

"Stone-Cold Predators"

To cite just a few examples, following my May 1995 address to the district attorneys association, big-city prosecutors inundated me with war stories about the ever-growing numbers of hardened, remorseless juveniles who were showing up in the system. "They kill or maim on impulse, without any intelligible motive," said one. Likewise, a veteran beat policeman confided: "I never used to be scared. Now I say a quick Hail Mary every time I get a call at night involving juveniles. I pray I go home in one piece to my own kids."

On a visit to a New Jersey maximum-security prison, I spoke to a group of life-term inmates, many of them black males from inner-city Newark and Camden. In a typical remark, one prisoner fretted, "I was a bad-ass street gladiator, but these kids are stone-cold predators." Likewise, in his just-published book, Mansfield B. Frazier, a five-time convicted felon, writes of what he calls "The Coming Menace": "As bad as conditions are in many of our nation's ravaged inner-city neighborhoods, in approximately five years they are going to get worse, a lot worse." Having done time side-by-side with today's young criminals in prisons and jails all across the country, he warns of a "sharp, cataclysmic" increase in youth crime and violence.

To add my own observations to this pile, since 1980 I've studied prisons and jails all across the country—San Quentin, Leavenworth, Rikers Island. I've been on the scene at prison murders and riots (and once was almost killed inside a prison). Moreover, I grew up in a pretty tough neighborhood and am built like an aging linebacker. I will still waltz backwards, notebook in hand and alone, into any adult maximum-security cellblock full of killers, rapists, and muggers.

But a few years ago, I forswore research inside juvenile lockups. The buzz of impulsive violence, the vacant stares and smiles, and the remorseless eyes were at once too frightening and too depressing (my God, these are *children!*) for me to pretend to "study" them.

Alarming Numbers

The numbers are as alarming as the anecdotes. At a time when overall crime rates have been dropping, youth crime rates, especially for crimes of violence, have been soaring. Between 1985 and 1992, the rate at which males ages 14 to 17 committed murder increased by about 50 percent for whites and over 300 percent for blacks.

While it remains true that most violent youth crime is committed by juveniles against juveniles, of late young offenders have been committing more homicides, robberies, and other crimes against adults. There is even some evidence that juveniles are doing homicidal violence in "wolf packs." Indeed, a 1993 study found that juveniles committed about a third of all homicides against strangers, often murdering their victim in groups of two or more.

109

Violent youth crime, like all serious crime, is predominantly *intra*-racial, not interracial. The surge in violent youth crime has been most acute among black inner-city males. In 1992, black males ages 16 to 19 experienced violent crime at nearly double the rate of white males and were about twice as likely to be violent crime victims as were black males in 1973. Moreover, the violent crimes experienced by young black males tended to be more serious than those experienced by young white males; for example, aggravated assaults rather than simple assaults, and attacks involving guns rather than weaponless violence.

The youth crime wave has reached horrific proportions from coast to coast. For example, in Philadelphia, more than half of the 433 people murdered in 1994 were males between the ages of 16 and 31. All but 5 of the 89 victims under 20 were non-white. In Los Angeles, there are now some 400 youth street gangs organized mainly along racial and ethnic lines: 200 Latino, 150 black, the rest white or Asian. In 1994, their known members alone committed 370 murders and over 3,300 felony assaults.

But what is really frightening everyone from D.A.s to demographers, old cops to old convicts, is not what's happening now but what's just around the corner—namely, a sharp increase in the number of super crime-prone young males.

Nationally, as of 1995 there are about 40 million children under the age of 10, the largest number in decades. By simple math, in 2005 today's 4- to 7-year-olds will have become 14- to 17-year-olds. By 2005, the number of males in this age group will have risen about 25 percent overall and 50 percent for blacks.

To some extent, it's just that simple: More boys begets more bad boys. But to really grasp why this spike in the young male population means big trouble ahead, you need to appreciate both the statistical evidence from a generation of birth-cohort studies and related findings from recent street-level studies and surveys.

6 Percent Do 50 Percent

The scientific kiddie-crime literature began with a study of all 10,000 boys born in 1945 who lived in Philadelphia between their tenth and eighteenth birthdays. Over one-third had at least one recorded arrest by the time they were 18. Most of the arrests occurred when the boys were ages 15 to 17. Half of the boys who were arrested were arrested more than once. Once a boy had been arrested three times, the chances that he would be arrested again were over 70 percent.

But the most famous finding of the study was that 6 percent of the boys committed five or more crimes before they were 18, accounting for over half of all the serious crimes, and about two-thirds of all the violent crimes, committed by the entire cohort.

This "6 percent do 50 percent" statistic has been replicated in

110

a series of subsequent longitudinal studies of Philadelphia and many other cities. It is on this basis that James Q. Wilson and other leading crime doctors can predict with confidence that the additional 500,000 boys who will be 14 to 17 years old in the year 2000 will mean at least 30,000 more murderers, rapists, and muggers on the streets than we have today.

Likewise, it's what enables California officials to meaningfully predict that, as the state's population of 11- to 17-year-olds grows from 2.9 million in 1993 to 3.9 million in 2004, the number of juvenile arrests will increase nearly 30 percent.

But that's only half the story. The other half begins with the less well-known but equally important and well-replicated finding that since the studies began, each generation of crime-prone boys (the "6 percent") has been about three times as dangerous as the one before it. For example, crime-prone boys born in Philadelphia in 1958 went on to commit about three times as much serious crime per capita as their older cousins in the class of '45. Thus, the difference between the juvenile criminals of the 1950s and those of the 1970s and 80s was about the difference between the Sharks and Jets of *West Side Story* fame and the Bloods and Crips of Los Angeles County.

The Theory of Moral Poverty

Still, demography is not fate and criminology is not pure science. How can one be certain that the demographic bulge will unleash an army of young male predatory street criminals who will make even the leaders of the Bloods and Crips—known as O.G.s, for "original gangsters"—look tame by comparison?

The answer centers on a conservative theory of the root causes of crime, one that is strongly supported by all of the best science as well as the common sense of the subject. Call it the theory of moral poverty.

Most Americans of every race, religion, socioeconomic status, and demographic description grow up in settings where they are taught right from wrong and rewarded emotionally or spiritually (if not also or always materially) for deferring immediate gratification and respecting others. Most of us were blessed to be born to loving and responsible parents or guardians. And most of us were lucky enough to have other adults in our lives (teachers, coaches, clergy) who reinforced the moral lessons that we learned at home—don't be selfish, care about others, plan for the future, and so on.

But some Americans grow up in moral poverty. Moral poverty is the poverty of being without loving, capable, responsible adults who teach you right from wrong. It is the poverty of being without parents and other authorities who habituate you to feel joy at others' joy, pain at others' pain, happiness when you

111

do right, remorse when you do wrong. It is the poverty of growing up in the virtual absence of people who teach morality by
their own everyday example and who insist that you follow suit.

In the extreme, moral poverty is the poverty of growing up
surrounded by deviant, delinquent, and criminal adults in abusive, violence-ridden, fatherless, Godless, and jobless settings.
In sum, whatever their material circumstances, kids of whatever race, creed, or color are most likely to become criminally
depraved when they are morally deprived.

Most predatory street criminals—black and white, adult and juvenile, past and present—have grown up in abject moral poverty.
But the Bloods and Crips were so much more violent, on average, than their 50s counterparts, and the next class of juvenile
offenders will be even worse, because in recent decades each
generation of youth criminals in this country has grown up in
more extreme conditions of moral poverty than the one before it.

Early Beginnings

The abject moral poverty that creates super-predators begins
very early in life in homes where unconditional love is nowhere
but unmerciful abuse is common. One of the best ethnographic
accounts of this reality is Mark S. Fleisher's 1995 book on the
lives of 194 West Coast urban street criminals, including several
dozen who were juveniles at the time he did his primary field
research (1988 to 1990). Almost without exception, the boys'
families "were a social fabric of fragile and undependable social
ties that weakly bound children to their parents and other so-
cializers." Nearly all parents abused alcohol or drugs or both.
Most had no father in the home; many had fathers who were
criminals. Parents "beat their sons and daughters—whipped
them with belts, punched them with fists, slapped them, and
kicked them."

Such ethnographic evidence is mirrored by national statistics
on the morally impoverished beginnings of incarcerated populations. For example, 75 percent of highly violent juvenile criminals suffered serious abuse by a family member; nearly 80 percent witnessed extreme violence (beatings, killings); over half of
prisoners come from single-parent families; over one-quarter
have parents who abused drugs or alcohol; nearly a third have a
brother with a prison or jail record.

Among other puzzles, the moral poverty theory explains why,
despite living in desperate economic poverty, under the heavy
weight of Jim Crow, and with plenty of free access to guns, the
churchgoing, two-parent black families of the South never experienced anything remotely like the tragic levels of homicidal
youth and gang violence that plague some of today's black inner-
city neighborhoods.

112

It also explains why once relatively crime-free white working-class neighborhoods are evolving into white underclass neighborhoods. The out-migration of middle-class types, divorce, out-of-wedlock births, and graffiti-splattered churches have spawned totally unsocialized young white males who commit violent crimes and youth gangs that prefer murder to mischief (anyone who doubts it is welcome to tour my old Catholic blue-collar neighborhood in Philadelphia.)

Developmental Defects

Moral poverty begets juvenile super-predators whose behavior is driven by two profound developmental defects. First, they are radically present-oriented. Not only do they perceive no relationship between doing right (or wrong) now and being rewarded (or punished) for it later. They live entirely in and for the present moment; they quite literally have no concept of the future. As several researchers have found, ask a group of today's young big-city murderers for their thoughts about "the future," and many of them will ask you for an explanation of the question.

Second, the super-predators are radically self-regarding. They regret getting caught. For themselves, they prefer pleasure and freedom to incarceration and death. Under some conditions, they are affectionate and loyal to fellow gang members or relatives, but not even moms or grandmoms are sacred to them; as one prisoner quipped, "crack killed everybody's 'mama.'" And they place zero value on the lives of their victims, whom they reflexively dehumanize as just so much worthless "white trash" if white, or by the usual racial or ethnic epithets if black or Latino.

Super-Alones

We adults now name the young criminals super-predators. Perhaps we should think of them as the super-alones. There are children in America who have never been touched or told that they matter. Inner-city mama is on crack. Or suburban mama gives the nanny responsibility for raising the kids. Papa is in a rage this morning. Where are the aunts to protect the child? Where is there a neighbor who cares?

Richard Rodriguez, *Los Angeles Times*, January 21, 1996.

On the horizon, therefore, are tens of thousands of severely morally impoverished juvenile super-predators. They are perfectly capable of committing the most heinous acts of physical violence for the most trivial reasons (for example, a perception of slight disrespect or the accident of being in their path). They

113

fear neither the stigma of arrest nor the pain of imprisonment. They live by the meanest code of the meanest streets, a code that reinforces rather than restrains their violent, hair-trigger mentality. In prison or out, the things that super-predators get by their criminal behavior—sex, drugs, money—are their own immediate rewards. Nothing else matters to them. So for as long as their youthful energies hold out, they will do what comes "naturally": murder, rape, rob, assault, burglarize, deal deadly drugs, and get high.

No Serious Answers

What is to be done? I will conclude with one big idea, but my best advice is not to look for serious answers from either crowd in Washington.

Early in 1995, I was among a dozen guests invited to a working White House dinner on juvenile crime. Over gourmet Szechwan wonton and lamb, the meeting dragged on for three-and-a-half hours. President Clinton took copious notes and asked lots of questions, but nothing was accomplished. One guest pleaded with him to declare a National Ceasefire Day. Wisely, he let that one pass. But another guest recommended that he form (you guessed it) a commission. In mid-July, the president named six members to a National Commission on Crime Control and Prevention. I didn't know whether to laugh or cry.

Meanwhile, Republicans have made some real improvements on the 1994 crime bill. But it is hard to imagine that block-granting anti-crime dollars will work (it never has before). And it is easy to see how the passion for devolution is driving conservatives to contradict themselves. For years they've stressed that drugs, crime, and welfare dependency are cultural and moral problems. Now, however, they talk as if perverse monetary incentives explained everything.

True, government policies helped wreck the two-parent family and disrupted other aspects of civil society. But how does the sudden withdrawal of government lead automatically to a rebirth of civil society, an end to moral poverty, and a check on youth crime? It doesn't, not any more than pulling a knife from the chest of a dead man brings him dancing back to life. Liberal social engineering was bad; conservative social re-engineering will prove worse.

Say "Amen"

My one big idea is borrowed from three well-known child-development experts—Moses, Jesus Christ, and Mohammed. It's called religion. If we are to have a prayer of stopping any significant fraction of the super-predators short of the prison gates, then we had better say "Amen," and fast.

Why religion? Two reasons. First, a growing body of scientific evidence from a variety of academic disciplines indicates that churches can help cure or curtail many severe socioeconomic ills. For example, a 1986 study by Harvard economist Richard Freeman found that among black urban youth, church attendance was a better predictor of who would escape drugs, crime, and poverty than any other single variable (income, family structure) and that churchgoing youth were more likely than otherwise comparable youth to behave in socially constructive ways. Likewise, a study by a panel of leading specialists just published by the journal *Criminology* concluded that, while much work remains to be done, there is substantial empirical evidence that religion serves "as an insulator against crime and delinquency." And we have long known that many of the most effective substance-abuse prevention and treatment programs, both in society and behind bars, are either explicitly religious or quasi-religious in their orientation.

Second, religion is the one answer offered time and again by the justice-system veterans, prisoners, and others I've consulted. With particular reference to black youth crime, for example, it is an answer proffered in books by everyone from liberal Cornel West to neoconservative Glenn Loury, Democrat Jesse Jackson to Republican Alan Keyes.

In a recent forum at Trenton's Mount Zion AME Church, Isaac "Ike" Ballard, executive director of education for the New Jersey prison system, spoke the big truth: "The church is the most potent establishment in every black community. It is the single entity that can take on the mission of economic development and give people, especially young people, an alternative to drugs and crime." To be sure, black churches are in decline in many needy neighborhoods. They are straining to stay open despite lost membership, near-empty coffers, and increasing community demands. Still, they remain the last best hope for rebuilding the social and spiritual capital of inner-city America.

Empower the Churches

We must, therefore, be willing to use public funds to empower local religious institutions to act as safe havens for at-risk children (church-run orphanages, boarding schools, call them what you please), provide adoption out-placement services, administer government-funded "parenting skills" classes, handle the youngest non-violent juvenile offenders, provide substance-abuse treatment, run day-care and pre-school programs, and perform other vital social and economic development functions.

Although many government officials are reluctant to admit it—and while data on how much of each government social-services dollar already goes through religious institutions are in-

115

credibly sparse—in some places churches are already performing such tasks with direct or indirect public support. We should enable them to do even more.

Obviously, even with increased public support, churches could not come close to saving every child or solving every social problem. But I'd bet that the marginal return on public investments that strengthen the community-rebuilding and child-protection capacities of local churches would equal or exceed that of the marginal tax dollar spent on more cops, more public schools, and more prisons.

Such proposals raise all sorts of elite hackles. But most Americans believe in God (90 percent) and pray each day (80 percent). The trouble is that our faith in God and religion is not reflected in federal, state, and local social policies, courtesy of the anti-religious and non-religious liberal and conservative pseudo-sophisticates of both parties. Let them argue church-state issues (anyone remember the Northwest Ordinance or what the Founding Fathers really said about religion?) all the way to the next funeral of an innocent kid caught in the crossfire. Let these theoretic politicians, as Madison would disparagingly call them, trifle with non-issues concerning which level of government ought to take the lead in protecting lives and property. (Answer: all.)

No one in academia is a bigger fan of incarceration than I am. Between 1985 and 1991 the number of juveniles in custody increased from 49,000 to nearly 58,000. By my estimate, we will probably need to incarcerate at least 150,000 juvenile criminals in the years just ahead. In deference to public safety, we will have little choice but to pursue genuine get-tough law-enforcement strategies against the super-predators.

But some of these children are now still in diapers, and they can be saved. So let our guiding principle be, "Build churches, not jails"—or we will reap the whirlwind of our own moral bankruptcy.

Periodical Bibliography

The following articles have been selected to supplement the diverse views presented in this chapter. Addresses are provided for periodicals not indexed in the *Readers' Guide to Periodical Literature*, the *Alternative Press Index*, or the *Social Sciences Index*.

David Elkind	"What Happens When Markers of Maturity Disappear?" *Education Digest*, January 1989.
J. Kirschenbaum	"More Cuts to Kids: Anti-Prostitution Budget Axed," *City Limits*, May 1995.
Nicholas Lemann	"The Vogue of Childhood Misery," *Atlantic Monthly*, March 1992.
Terrie E. Moffitt	"Measuring Children's Antisocial Behaviors," *JAMA*, February 7, 1996. Available from the American Medical Association, Box 10945, Chicago, IL 60610.
James Moore	"Addressing a Hidden Problem: Kansas Youth Center Treats Sexually Abused Female Offenders," *Corrections Today*, February 1991. Available from 4380 Forbes Blvd., Lanham, MD 20706-4322.
Newsweek	"What Kind of Child Would Kill a Child?" March 1, 1993.
C. Nowakowski	"Guns and Comic Books," *Chartist*, July 1995.
Andrew O'Hagan	"Growing Up Nasty," *Harper's*, June 1993.
Amy Pagnozzi	"When Good Kids Kill," *New York*, October 23, 1995.
Psychology Today	"Primed for Crime," July/August 1993.
Anne Richardson Roiphe	"The Hatred Behind Sexual Aggression," *Glamour*, April 1993.
Jeremy Seabrook	"Crime and the Paradoxes of Consumerism," *Toward Freedom*, March 1995.
E.R. Shipp, Felicia R. Lee, and Mary B.W. Tabor	"Life at 'Jeff': Tough Students Wonder Where Childhood Went," *New York Times*, March 7, 1992.
Don Terry	"When the Family Heirloom Is Homicide," *New York Times*, December 12, 1994.
World Press Review	"Children Who Kill," June 1993.

What Factors Contribute to Gang-Related Juvenile Crime?

Juvenile
Crime

Chapter Preface

Law enforcement officials and social service experts offer numerous explanations for why young people join gangs. One common argument is that many youths are attracted to gangs because they come from "broken" families—usually families from which the father is absent. According to John Williams Jr., a community outreach worker in Colorado, "Most gang-involved youths come from single-parent homes. . . . They often turn to people in the street because their family isn't meeting their needs of love, communication and support." Laron Douglas, a member of the Gangster Disciples, describes this experience: "I grew up without a father and I turned to my Disciple brothaz for love. They knew exactly how to treat a brotha and were always there for me, through thick and thin."

Others insist that in the violent environment of many inner cities, youths have little choice but to join a gang. Their safety—even their survival—may depend on being associated with and protected by fellow gang members. Albert McGee, a member of the Insane Vice Lords, writes, "Contrary to popular belief, I didn't join because I lacked a family. For me, it was simply a matter of my surroundings. . . . On the streets I'm just another gangbanger trying to survive the war."

Besides emotional support and a means of survival, gangs also offer promises of excitement, status, and financial gain resulting from drug dealing and other criminal activities. The various factors that contribute to gang-related juvenile crime and violence are examined in the following chapter.

1 VIEWPOINT

"We've been deprived of a lot of things: civil rights and basic humanity."

Racism Contributes to Gang-Related Crime

Baby Nerve, Jason Belok, Nate II, and Spud, interviewed by Sharin Elkholy and Ahmed Nassef

The 1992 Los Angeles riots erupted after four white police officers were acquitted of charges of police brutality in the beating of black motorist Rodney King. Many commentators charged that gang members within the African-American community premeditated and instigated the violence and destruction of property that occurred during the riots. In the following viewpoint, Sharin Elkholy and Ahmed Nassef interview gang members Baby Nerve, Jason Belok, Nate II, and Spud shortly after the National Guard arrived on the scene of the rioting. All four gang members maintain that the pervasive racism in American society leads young people of color to vent their frustration through gang-related crime and violence such as the riots. Elkholy is an independent producer. Nassef was a graduate student at UCLA at the time this interview was conducted.

As you read, consider the following questions:

1. What reason does Nerve give for being frustrated with "the white man's system"?
2. How does Spud view the Rodney King beating? How does he describe his own experience with the Los Angeles police?
3. Who does Spud say he is referring to with the phrase "the system"?

Excerpted from "Crips and Bloods Speak for Themselves: Voices from South Central," *Against the Current*, July/August 1992, transcribed from the original KPFK radio interview on May 15, 1992. Reprinted by permission of *Against the Current* and the Pacifica Foundation, owner of station KPFK, Los Angeles. For a copy of the tape, call 1-800-735-0230.

Ahmed: *How do you feel about the overwhelming police and military presence in your community?*

Nerve: Yes, Black people are out there looting, yes Black people burnt down buildings. It might have been Koreans and white people that burnt down their own buildings just to get money from insurance. People need to figure out how the government works, how the system is, before they come and try to pass judgement and call us these different names such as gangsters, looters, Bloods, Crips, thugs and thieves.

We are Black people, we are Mexican, we are Japanese and we are even dirty little white people—you know what I'm saying. You all got to figure out who you are, where you come from, and what's your foundation in life. As of today's society, we're accepting the white man's way of living, we're not living by our own ways. And we got to find out where our feet come from, our soil.

We have to have knowledge, wisdom and understanding of our past and our culture, because your culture is your freedom. We have to find out the truth so we can refine ourselves from this white man's ways.

Build and Destroy

Ahmed: *When you referred to whites, you called them "dirty little white people," there's obviously anger there.*

Nerve: It's frustration with the white man's system. They created the system. They made the laws. They wrote the constitution. We didn't have any say in it, we're just people living in their society in which they try to control us in every which way. They bring drugs into the community and give it to us, then the people selling drugs, they put them in jail and say they were wrong. But you bring the drugs into our community.

Spud: We ain't got no coca plants in our backyards, they don't grow in the U.S. Just like when they brought us over here—we didn't want to come over here. We didn't know nothing about war when we came over here, we learned all our ways from the white man. Cause this is their world, we're just living in it. Now you say it's over, the looting and the fires, but it's not over until we make a change. It's like Little Monster said: It's time to break it down and build it up.

Nerve: Build and destroy. We're going to build ourselves and we're going to destroy their system. That's what we want to do.

Spud: It needs to get fair. Until you can treat us all like you treat the people in Simi Valley [the white community where the police officers accused of beating Rodney King were tried], it ain't gonna stop. The violence, as far as looting or whatever is gonna stop, but we're not gonna sit down and be passive and just let what they say go. We're gonna speak our mind, we're gonna

121

protest, we're gonna do whatever we have to do in a positive way, or if it has to be in a negative way, to get our point across. We're tired. This Rodney King incident wasn't the first thing—it was just the straw that broke the camel's back. It just let us know it's time to get started. The looting and the fires, that was frustration let out by the Black community as a whole.

Unfairly Branded as Criminals

In the common image of the urban thug, a dark-skinned youth wears baggy clothes, heavy jewelry, and a menacing expression. This picture, popularized in movies and music videos, has begun to show up in police department practice manuals—along with other characteristics—as the "profile" of the typical urban gang member.

To combat violent street gangs, many law enforcement agencies have developed "gang profiles" to identify young people as members or associates of gangs. The criteria range from known criminal activity and admitted gang membership to style of dress, tattoos, favorite hangouts, and the identities of friends. Some businesses have adopted similar profiles as a way to screen out potentially troublesome customers. . . .

Civil rights advocates claim that police are casting too wide a net in a fishing expedition that sweeps in innocent people—primarily young minority men—who happen to fit the broad stereotype of a gang member.

Allegedly based on profiles, teens have been thrown out of shopping malls, ejected from amusement parks, and stopped and searched by police, who may later enter their names and photos into computer databases. Their lawyers have filed lawsuits on their behalf, claiming that racial and other biases have unfairly branded these young people as criminals.

Julie Gannon Shoop, *Trial*, October 1994.

Ahmed: *So you're saying it wasn't just a bunch of "thugs" or a bunch of "hoodlums" arbitrarily destroying things. There's a political message to what is happening—this was a real uprising.*

Nerve: Yes, it's a point that people made. People are out there with no jobs, there's people out there hungry. It's Blacks, Mexicans . . .

Spud: People of color.

Nerve: People of color just out there with no jobs, you know what I'm saying. Okay [if] you got some money in the bank, you can keep on rollin'—you know the government will give you a loan.

Spud: How many gang members do you know that can get a loan.

Nerve: How many gang members do you know that can get out of jail and say, I want to start me a business and get me a loan. You don't have none. The government is so crooked, the Koreans don't understand—the government gave you a loan and put you in our community to set you up for this. Yes, you're in our community. You got tooken just like we got tooken.

Spud: So the frustration get took out on the Korean instead of the white man.

Nate: You know we've been deprived of a lot of things: civil rights and basic humanity. I want to let people know that it's a diversion, they want us to focus on the Korean and the Black issue, which is not really a Korean and a Black issue. It's a Black and a white issue, it's a minority and a white issue.

The media was so biased. I get so frustrated when I turn on the idiot box—that's what I call my television. I have to take everything they say and put it in proper context because it's not a Korean/Black thing; the merchants were there, there were problems, but it's a diversion to get us not to think about the real problem, which is the oppressor, which is the major majority which are whites.

They want to say that the Korean-Americans and the Black-Americans are feuding and having gun fights in the streets. This has been going on for years and years. But the whole focus is the trial, civil rights, humanity, fairness . . . that's it.

Spud: Equality.

Equality Is the Biggest Thing

Nerve: Equality is the biggest thing that people don't understand. Equality. See, the white man has all the money. They have all the control. They tax us, they tax our dollar so they can put their money where they want to put it. They put their money back into drugs. How you gonna give another country money, but you can't give us no money. How you gonna take our tax money and give it to somebody else when we ask for it for our community and you can't give it to us.

Belok: They say that's the system, but where does the system concern us? The system's not benefiting us, it's benefiting them.

Nate: I believe throughout the whole incident, throughout the whole rebellion, America's mass media is painting a bad picture of gang members and Blacks. People that were out there looting and stealing and robbing weren't out there because there was nothing to do on a Wednesday and a Thursday. They were angry. They were angry from years of deprivation coming to a head, it was just the tip of the iceberg. Right now we're trying to plead to all young Black males and females that are in gangs or associated with gangs to come together, united we stand divided we fall.

Ahmed: *Come together and do what?*

Nerve: Come together and understand, form a political party if that's what it takes. Wake up! and find out who is your enemy. Just like they say, your enemy could be a Black man in your organization who is going out and telling the white folk your plans. What we're saying is come together, find some peace, find out what we need to do to break the system down. That's all we want. We want the whole world to understand that equality is the basic thing. We want the whole world to understand that we're not taking this no more.

Spud: The Bloods and the Crips can squash their beefs and realize that we're not the enemy. We're not the common enemy as we thought we were. We can wake up and keep this on our minds and realize we got a bigger and worse enemy then ourselves, because we're not enemies at all.

Patrol Buddies

The Los Angeles communities are demanding that they are policed and patrolled by individuals who live in the community and the commanding officers be ten-year residents of the community in which they serve. Former gang members shall be given a chance to be patrol buddies in assisting in the protection of the neighborhoods. These former gang members will be required to go through police training and must comply to all of the laws instituted by our established authorities. Uniforms will be issued to each and every member of the "buddy system," however, no weapons will be issued. . . . Each buddy patrol will be supplied with a video camera and will tape each event and the officers handling the police matter. The buddy patrol will not interfere with any police matter unless instructed by a commanding officer.

The Bloods and Crips, from their post-riot plan for rebuilding South Central Los Angeles, excerpted in the *Nation*, June 1, 1992.

Ahmed: *Last week, would you have been able to stand here together, the Crips and the Bloods, different colors standing in one room together? How new is this and is it going to last?*

Spud: This is new and it's going to last because we want it to last, and we're gonna do whatever it takes to make it last. If the little peons in certain Bloods and Crips organizations don't want it to last and want to keep drama comin', we're gonna squash them because we're not gonna let them control this. We're gonna control this ourselves, and think and keep our minds strong the whole time so we can overcome all of this.

Ahmed: *On the streets there are a bunch of National Guardsmen with their M-16 rifles. What's going to happen if they stay on the streets another week, another month? Are people going to allow this to happen, or is there going to be some sort of response from the community?*

Nate: The show of force by the government is only there to pacify. It's there so the white people can turn on their television set and say we're keeping the Blacks in line. That's why the media and that's why [George] Bush and [Daryl] Gates and the Mayor have all put that together: to give them a sense that everything's all going back to normal. It's not!

Spud: How fair is that? How fair is that for them to have over 9,000 or somethin' arrests and when their seventy-two hours before seeing a judge is up, all of a sudden the Governor and Bush pass down a new law to give it a week. How fair is that? But if the majority of the 9,000 would have been white, they would have been out of there in seventy-two hours when their rights were violated. Our rights are violated so now they make a new law. It just proves more and more that it's not fair and we're not going to stand for it or sit by and accept this no more.

Manipulated by the System

Ahmed: *People are being told by the media that there is an African-American leadership—people like Jesse Jackson and Reverend Cecil Murray at the AME [African Methodist Episcopal] Church who are asking for people to stop the violence, looting and burning. Are these people your leaders?*

Spud: They're spokesmen for certain parts of the Black community, or maybe as a whole. They want the violence stopped. We want the violence stopped. We're not here to promote violence; just because we're gang members and we've been caught up in this train of thought for so long, it doesn't necessarily mean we're here to promote violence. We're here to promote unity with our Black community, that's all we want—equality and fairness.

Nerve: See, right now we're the leaders. If they want to speak to us, they've got to get with us right now. If you want to know what the gang members think and how we feel, this is where we are. We're on the streets, we're not in the church. We don't go to church with a suit on every Sunday. We're the ones who have been manipulated by the system. You guys [African-American leadership establishment] are political and the government ain't gonna touch you because you're doing exactly what they want you to do.

Spud: You're the little percent they like—that will talk nice. But we're here to tell you the real. We're gonna tell you how we feel, what we're tired of, what we want, and how we plan to get it. And that's by any means necessary.

Belok: For the people that didn't understand and that just looked at us as violent people, just imagine this: Just imagine if the Rodney King incident wasn't captured on videotape. Who was he gonna turn to? Who is he going to tell, the sergeant, or someone that was probably there hitting him with a billy club fifty times?

Spud: That happens every day, there's nothing new about that. That's common law—especially to gang members. They [the police] abuse us, they come and smack you just because you got on a burgundy shirt, "come here nigger," callin' me all types of slang names and disrespecting me, making me feel less than human just because I choose to wear a certain color.

Ahmed: *So that's normal procedure for the L.A.P.D. [Los Angeles Police Department].*

Spud: That's normal procedure daily. They look at you like dirt, they talk to you like dirt. This Rodney King incident ain't nothin' new, this time it was able to be seen on videotape. And it still wasn't no good 'cause they got off free, so that shows you the injustice in this system.

Bad Press

Ahmed: *What do you think about the media and the propaganda campaign that seems to be going on showing the people sweeping the streets, many of them white people?*

Nate: I think that's very necessary. You have to have a cleanup process—nobody is knocking that. You have to get things done. Debris has to be moved. Maybe those people are genuine in their feelings and thoughts and that's why they come down here to help the community. Everyone's not evil per se. It's not like the media says where gang members hate all white people. It's not really like that. All a person really wants to do is focus on the points after the cleaning up is done. What about the reconstruction? Are we gonna be the first ones there?

Belok: You got to get out here and get to the root of the problem and understand and communicate and know what's really on people's minds. You can't just get on the news and think or assume what you want to think.

Nate: Now if you get some people that's already pissed off and there's no police around and they see some people taking stuff for free and they ain't got no money, what's next? This whole thing was fueled by the media. Everything that happened in South Central Los Angeles was fueled by the media. When they had a chance to go focus on the churches and the peaceful rallies which were going on (and you know sometimes I feel you got to get off your knees sometime and dust them off and get out there and do something).

But the whole thing, I want to put it in a nutshell: it's KABC's fault, ABC's fault, and CBS. They're the people that hyped up the rebellion. I don't know if it's a money thing. I don't really understand the system—all I know is I'm a victim of it.

How Whites Can Help

Spud: Some people are genuine with their sincerity and that's good. When we say the white man is doing this, we're not talking about the whole Caucasian population as a whole. Just the system—the ones in power. They're the white people we're talking about. We're not racist and we're not prejudiced 'cause we know how it feels to be on the receiving end of prejudice.

Why do we want to turn around and let another person, human being, white, Korean, or whatever, feel all the pain and hurt that we've been through? We don't. We just want them to see and realize that it's not fair.

Ahmed: *What do you tell a white person who is living in Santa Monica or Pacific Palisades, who usually knows little about the African community and who may not have even been to South Central or East L.A. and who wants to do something to help? What can they do to help?*

Nerve: They can organize their community, their white community, and fight against what's going on. They have to fight their war and we have to fight our war and we'll all go against the system.

Spud: People should be living in happiness. We don't need to continue to go through poverty and problems, racist problems or any other type of problem that's detrimental to us. Ask yourself—is it really fair? Would you like what's happening to us on a daily basis to happen to you? Would you like to be called a punk white boy just because you chose to wear a red or a blue shirt? Just because the media hypes up gang members as mindless senseless killers who just ride by and shoot innocent children?

I never met a gang member, Crip or Blood, in my life that purposely tried to hurt an innocent baby. But look who's got the biggest gang in the world—the military. Who drops bombs and kills millions of babies in other countries—the military. Who's the military run by—the white man, the system.

Ahmed: *Are you registered to vote and do you perceive change occurring through the present system?*

Nerve: I have no reason to vote. Why should I vote for George Bush or [Bill] Clinton when they don't do anything but bring drugs into our community? They don't do nothing but send our people to war. The government is a big cover-up. I have no need to vote for none of them. They ain't doin' nothing for me. They ain't walkin' on the streets tellin' me to stop the violence.

They're not down here where we are. They're in some big old white building talking about White House, white system and let's try and do something to contain these Black people—let's try and do something to control the world.

Wherever there are people of color, they're in the same predicament as we are. No matter if it's Mexico, Afghanistan, Iran—the white man is living in his big old house and all he does is point his finger and send his troops and try to control that country while he's sitting up fat.

Spud: They have our people so confused thinking that everything he's [the white man] doing is the right thing. When he's just hurting their culture, their heritage, the other Black brothers and sisters in the community. We're still a part of them whether they like it or not, no matter what they feel we do, or their opinions or assumptions of us.

Recycling the System

Nerve: We're talking about breaking the system down. We want to take all that paper that you got, all those laws you got, we want them burnt up. We want that paper recycled.

Spud: Exactly, recycled!

Nerve: The system has been so wicked for so many years, and there's no candidate that's running for office that is going to do anything for the Black community, but I am registered to vote. But it doesn't really mean anything for us.

Ahmed: *We're standing at Masjid Al Saff, a Muslim Mosque in Inglewood. Why are you here? What role does Islam play for you?*

Belok: We want to be heard, simple as that. We want people to understand what's really going on, instead of thinking that we're bad so they have an excuse for doing something like the Rodney King incident.

Spud: I'm here with the Muslims because their beliefs are basically what I believe in, what I want, what we want to fight for. And they're backing us and advising us. We all want the same common goal . . . peace.

Nerve: You got probably a million churches out there and what do you see them doing?

Spud: The Black churches are happy that we're out here still getting abused and beat up, because they feel they safe. They safe regardless. We don't want to hurt them. We don't want to hurt no other Black elderly. We don't want to hurt their children. We don't want to hurt nobody, we just want to be treated fairly. And they're happy that the white man, the system, has sent down armies to contain us to keep them out of danger. They ain't never been in danger in the first place. You joining the person that's really keeping you in danger, the system, that's who you need to speak out against.

Nerve: The African Muslims come and talk to you as if you're a person. They give you respect as a person. They don't look down upon you, well you wear red, you wear blue, you're a Crip or you're a Blood. They don't call you no name, they don't call you no thug, they give you respect as a man.

Spud: And that's all we want is respect. Treat us like you treat everyone.

"Gangs and gang crime increase as economic opportunities decline."

Poverty Contributes to Gang-Related Crime

Donna Hunzeker

While not all youth gangs commit serious crimes, those that do tend to proliferate in communities that are economically depressed, Donna Hunzeker argues in the following viewpoint. According to Hunzeker, rates of gang-related crime are highest in areas of high unemployment and low income. She maintains that for adolescents in these communities, illegal gang activity can offer financial and social opportunities that otherwise appear unavailable to them. Hunzeker serves as the criminal justice expert for the National Conference of State Legislatures.

As you read, consider the following questions:

1. What needs do gangs fulfill for young adolescent males, in Hunzeker's view?
2. According to the author, what are the differences among "predatory gangs," "instrumental gangs," and "hedonistic gangs"?
3. What must be included in states' efforts to rebuild their economies, according to Richard Katz, as cited by Hunzeker?

Excerpted from Donna Hunzeker, "Ganging Up Against Violence," *State Legislatures*, May 1993; ©1993 by the National Conference of State Legislatures. Reprinted by permission of the conference.

While fires smoldered in riot-torn sections of Los Angeles in 1992, observers blamed police incompetence, pervasive poverty and resonating racism. Also blamed were juvenile gangs, whose members reportedly were responsible for much of the violence and who have become a feared personification of the urban underclass in this country.

The riots in South-Central Los Angeles subsided, but gang violence goes on. Incidents like the shooting death late in 1992 of a gang rival outside the church memorial service for another youth illustrate how grim life and death can be in gang communities. While Los Angeles continues to have the most disturbing amount of gang crime, cities across the country now report the existence of gangs and accompanying violence.

The number of juvenile gang members and how much crime they commit are subject to debate. Different definitions of gangs and gang crime are used in tracking and research. Record-keeping systems also vary, as does the way the data are interpreted.

Gang experts say that cities and especially police departments go through distinct stages of acknowledgment of and response to gang problems. The first recognizable stage often is "denial"—an unwillingness to tarnish the city's image and cause public fear by acknowledging their existence. On the other hand, where serious crimes have spurred reaction, officials may put many youths and youth crimes under a blanket definition of gangs, comparatively overstating the problem.

A national survey of law enforcement jurisdictions tallied nearly a quarter of a million gang members and more than 46,000 "gang incidents" in 1991. Of the 72 largest cities reporting, almost 20,000 violent offenses were attributed to gangs, including 974 homicides. The study, conducted by West Virginia University for the U.S. Department of Justice, said gang members predominantly are black and Hispanic. The numbers of white and Asian-American gang members were reported as far fewer, but on the rise.

A growing body of knowledge about gangs, including why they exist, who belongs to them, how they operate and how to solve their associated problems, is like the numbers, subject to varying interpretations. There is considerable consensus that gangs are tied to poverty and related social problems. The availability of drugs and especially weapons seems to increase gang members' propensity for crime and violence.

A Symptom of Poverty

Gang members overwhelmingly belong to an urban minority underclass. Research suggests that gangs and gang crime increase as economic opportunities decline. Ronald Huff, who directs the Criminal Justice Research Center at Ohio State Univer-

131

sity, has documented the fact that as manufacturing jobs were lost and unemployment rose in "rust belt" cities, low-income areas became fertile ground for juvenile gangs.

"An economically and socially marginal youth, who has dropped out of school or been expelled and is without job skills, is in deep trouble in Cleveland or Columbus," Huff reports. He and other researchers have noted that where neighborhoods, schools and families have decayed or dispersed, youths look for other means of esteem-building and social identity. Gang association and crime become attractive options where legitimate economic opportunities are lacking and social order is weak. Typical gang activities mirror the need for economic and social identity.

Gang Members in 1991 by Ethnicity

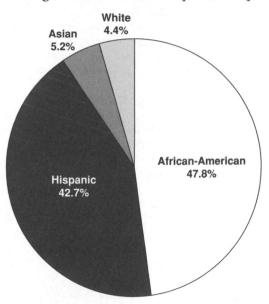

Source: National Institute of Justice, *Gang Crime and Law Enforcement Recordkeeping*, August 1994.

"Gang traditions have been crafted to satisfy precisely those needs which ache most powerfully in the souls of outcast adolescent males," writes Los Angeles District Attorney Ira Reiner in a 1992 report on gang crime and violence. Such traditions include passing a tough physical initiation, strong group identity and camaraderie, and a readiness to defend honor and turf.

Contrary to popular image, most gangs are rather loose associations of crime-prone young men forming a "surrogate family," according to Huff. They may wear colors and other insignia of Crips or Bloods, but they tend to be small, autonomous cliques. In Los Angeles, Reiner says, cliques average around four or five members—"roughly a car-load."

Gang members spend a good deal of their time engaging in exaggerated versions of typical adolescent behavior, according to Huff, who is interviewing gang members in six cities for the National Institute of Justice. Rebelling against authority, listening to loud music, hanging out and drinking alcohol or getting high are typical gang activities. Being a good, aggressive fighter also is an important reputation-builder for young gang members. "Fighting and partying" are the main occupations of gang members, says the Los Angeles district attorney.

Not All Gangs Are Alike

It is no misconception, however, that gang members commit many and often serious crimes. Experts distinguish members' drift into serious crime according to several gang types—distinctions that have policy implications as well.

"Predatory gangs," as identified by researcher Huff, commit the kinds of violent street crimes often associated with gangs—muggings, carjacking, rape and murder. These gang members often use drugs like crack cocaine, which contribute to violent, assaultive behavior. They also are likely to sell drugs, which pay for the sophisticated weapons they carry. Gang members often are readily available street dealers for organized cocaine cartels. Huff notes that lines start to blur between gangs and organized crime depending on the extent of involvement in organized drug trade. For some gang members, he says, "Color no longer is red or blue, but green."

Susan Pennell, who is directing a study of drug-involved gang members for the San Diego Association of Governments, says that while about three-quarters of gang members there sell drugs as a regular means of making money, only about one-third have sold drugs outside the county, a sign of higher-level involvement in the drug trade. It is not uncommon for older gang members to graduate into such drug-related criminality, researchers say. This trend appears to be accelerated by a weak economy and scarcity of legitimate jobs for young minority men.

"Instrumental gangs" tend to commit property crimes for money. Many members use drugs, including crack, and some sell drugs but not as an organized gang activity.

Finally, what Huff calls "hedonistic gangs" focus primarily on hanging out and getting high. Members commit minor property crimes, but not necessarily as a gang activity. Such gangs are not routinely involved in violent crime.

Almost any gang association carries with it the need for excitement and protection; therefore the propensity for violence is ever-present, says Pennell. "It should not surprise us that a group of young men who have drugs and guns and nothing to do would eventually wander into violent crime," she says.

Jobs Work

In my barrio, jobs, work and money saves lives. When I have had the funds to place a gang member on a job site and pay his salary, I've seen him stop banging. When, on the rarest of occasions, an employer has offered a job to one of these youth, I've witnessed kids suddenly have a reason to get up in the morning. Jobs fill them with a sense of purpose, pride and dignity. As much as I dislike the suggestion of single solutions to complex problems, jobs are as close as we will get to a single, effective answer to the enormous problem of gangs.

Gregory J. Boyle, *Los Angeles Times*, November 19, 1991.

Gang-related homicides usually are not random shootings or drug disputes, but rather the escalation of fights over turf, status or revenge, according to Reiner's analysis for the Los Angeles County district attorney's office. Drive-by shootings typically are committed by small sets of gang members, not entire gangs, and often are part of a chain reaction of vengeful events. Reiner says that one longtime gang battle among Crip factions in Los Angeles, to which he attributes two dozen deaths, started over a junior-high romance.

Pennell blames this kind of "ad lib violent crime" on the feeling of hopelessness that comes out of poverty paired with the availability of weapons. Interviews with some 200 gang members in San Diego reveal the same low regard for human life that other gang research has spoken of, Pennell says. "Many of these kids don't think they'll be alive at 25," she says. "And they accept that."

Gang Policy and Legislation

State legislation aimed at the gang problem has increased in recent years as gangs show up in cities and towns far from urban centers like Los Angeles and Chicago. Experts say that policy to deal with gangs needs to be centralized and comprehensive, pulling together all the systems involved and balancing the need for enforcement with prevention.

"A criminal justice response is very important, but by itself not very effective," says Winifred Reed, who manages gang search projects for the National Institute of Justice. Prevention, intervention and suppression all are necessary for controlling the impact of gangs, Reed says.

Huff recommends a two-pronged approach: 1) aggressive enforcement against hard-core "predatory" gang members; and 2) prevention directed at marginal and would-be gang members. Examples of both approaches are found in state laws.

Enforcement legislation in states like California, Nevada, Florida, Georgia and Illinois enhances penalties for crimes carried out in participation with or at the direction of gangs. The California Street Terrorism Enforcement and Protection Act of 1988, which other states have since emulated in name and spirit, makes it illegal to participate in a criminal street gang. It provides for an extra two or three years' imprisonment at the court's discretion for felonies committed in association with a gang. If the felony is punishable by life imprisonment, a minimum of 15 years must be served before parole is granted. Misdemeanor offenses committed in association with gangs also carry mandatory jail time. . . .

Programs for Kids Without Jobs

California followed up on its street terrorism act with a law that uses asset forfeiture funds for a Gang Risk Intervention Pilot (GRIP) program. The program includes individual and family counseling, cultural and recreational programs, job training and other activities to get at-risk kids interested in something other than drugs and gangs, according to Assemblyman Richard Katz, who represents the San Fernando Valley. . . .

Efforts to rebuild state economies and revitalize cities cannot overlook crime prevention, Katz says. There were more than 800 gang-related homicides in Los Angeles in 1992, a city heavily affected by the loss of 800,000 jobs in the state between 1990 and 1993.

States are finding other specialized means for funding gang prevention efforts. A "gangbuster bill" proposed by the Wisconsin Senate's assistant majority leader, Chuck Chvala, would create surcharges on weapon violations. These would fund police and gang prevention programs, including jobs programs that offer youths an incentive to get out of gangs, Chvala says. The Wisconsin bill also creates new penalties for drive-by shootings and gang recruitment, and enhanced penalties for gang-related crime.

Cities like Milwaukee, Madison and Green Bay are reporting gang problems that were unheard-of 10 years ago, Chvala says. Loss of manufacturing jobs in the area has diminished economic opportunity for many of the state's young people. "We cannot eliminate gangs unless we address the reasons they exist—hopelessness, joblessness and economic despair," he explains.

"The [drive-by] shootings examined here were not about drugs or gang territory. They were about guns, excitement, and an enhanced reputation."

A Desire for Excitement and Status Contributes to Gang-Related Crime

Roger H. Davis

In the following viewpoint, Roger H. Davis disputes the theory that gang-related drive-by shootings result from conflict between gangs over territory and drug markets. Davis presents the findings from a study of three drive-by shootings and concludes that such incidents stem from gang members' desire for excitement and status within their group. Davis, a retired FBI agent, is a private consultant in Fair Oaks, California.

As you read, consider the following questions:

1. What are two ways that gang members' desire for excitement incited drive-by shootings, according to Davis?
2. In the author's assessment, what roles did individual gang members perform in the drive-by shootings?
3. How did gang members behave after the shootings, according to Davis?

Excerpted from Roger H. Davis, "Cruising for Trouble," *FBI Law Enforcement Bulletin*, January 1995. Reprinted by permission.

- In San Diego, a 3-year-old child was shot.
- In Miami, it happened to a married couple.
- At Christmastime, even Santa became a victim.

A single factor connects these incidents; each involved a drive-by shooting by a gang member. Across the country, gang-related drive-by shootings are increasing at an alarming rate. Reports of bystanders injured by drive-by shootings frequently appear in the media, and many victims of these violent outbursts have no connection to gang activity. More frightening is the fact that no community appears to be immune, which leads to some very important questions.

What are the precipitating factors in drive-by shootings? Are they a result solely of drug or turf wars? Even more important, what, if anything, can be done about these incidents?

A 1994 study examined drive-by shootings and addressed these questions. The study focused on how individual gang members became involved in drive-by shootings, and the findings offer insight into the root causes of these incidents and the chain of events that precipitates such violent acts.

This viewpoint describes the patterns found among the three specific shootings studied. It then recommends steps for law enforcement agencies to take in an effort to prevent these violent episodes from happening in their communities.

The Study

Using case study methodology, three incidents were studied in great detail to identify factors that influenced gang members to participate in drive-by shootings. Case selection included black, Hispanic, and white gang-related, drive-by shootings. In all three cases, researchers documented reports of interactions among all participants and looked for patterns of involvement.

Three court cases in a medium-sized community formed the basis for the study. In each case, the responsible parties had been identified and charged, and the legal process had been completed. Because the cases were not selected randomly, the findings will not represent all drive-by shootings, but they do reveal the relationship between gang activities and drive-by shootings.

For each case, the research examined written police interview reports, transcripts of court testimony, and all available police audio and video recordings of interviews with the 79 participants. The cases were chosen, in part, because participants (shooters and others present before, during, and after the incidents) gave lengthy statements about their own and others' involvement. Some gave statements and/or testimony as often as times.

Shared Factors

Several factors consistently appeared in each drive-by shooting. First, all participants had committed criminal acts previously. Second, the gang's influence was significant in facilitating the incident. And third, the shootings were unplanned crimes of opportunity, although the participants admitted to looking for trouble and went out dressed for action.

Personal Background In all cases, the shooters identified with a youth gang. They came from dysfunctional families and had limited educational and employment experiences. Eighty-two percent of the participants had a history of involvement in serious crimes.

Desire for Excitement The gang members convened only to fight and cause trouble, and the shooters seized the opportunity to create an incident. Desire for excitement played a key role in turning each incident into a violent confrontation in two significant ways.

First, the desire for excitement provided momentum. The exchange of taunts, exaggeration of the threat posed by the rivals, and actual involvement in the incidents made gang members agitated and rowdy.

Security, Power, Excitement

Gang socialization processes vary by age, context, and situation, including access to alternative roles. Reasons for joining gangs include a need or wish for recognition, status, safety or security, power, excitement, and new experience. Youth raised under conditions of social deprivation are particularly drawn to gangs. Many youth view joining a gang as normal and respectable, even when the consequence is a series of delinquent and violent acts. Gang affiliation may constitute part of an expected socialization process in certain communities when they are viewed as embodying such values as honor, loyalty, and fellowship.

Irving Spergel et al., *Gang Suppression and Intervention: Problem and Response*, October 1994.

Second, the search for excitement facilitated arousal and motivated action. The participants who were interviewed explained they became exhilarated when preparing for battle, and this warrior mentality generated aggression. Gang members described the excitement that accompanies being ready to fight, and many saw themselves as soldiers ready to do battle with an adversary.

Alcohol and drug abuse also played a role in the search for excitement. In the cases studied, the individuals involved relie on their alcohol consumption and the drunken condition it spawned to rationalize their criminal acts.

Gang Identity Those involved in the shootings dressed in ways that marked them as gang members. In each case, participants signified gang affiliation through their clothing—red or blue baseball caps worn backwards, a blue rag exposed in a pocket, a certain color and type of shirt, or a jacket known as a "derby." Clothing and the exchange of hand signs communicated a challenge to potential rivals.

Shooting participants talked about gang symbols' being provocative and explained how the symbols of a larger gang organization implied power. One shooter admitted the importance of gang symbols when he stated, "We got to protect our colors." Gang members interpreted failure to show deference to the colors as an invitation to do battle. In fact, any sign of disrespect—the perceived affront from potential rivals or the exchange of stares or gang hand signs—warranted attack.

All gang members accepted the implied responsibility of being willing to commit a violent crime for the organization. When merely told of a conflict, one shooter saw an opportunity to "take care of this." Statements such as being "down to do a drive-by" for the gang implied gang members' sense of responsibility to protect and enhance the gang image as mercenaries in an elite corps. This behavior, which was designed to boost their egos and impress others, played a part in the process leading to violence.

Other Influences

Roles The gangs encouraged their most reactive and unpredictable members to take the initiative to shoot. No person acting on his own moved the events to violence. Instead, a combination of factors—including group pressure, certain members' desires to enhance their status, the availability of weapons, and previous confrontations—evoked the shootings.

In one case, the leader and an agitator worked together to build group support for a confrontation. They manipulated the shooter into a role that required him to take action. The shooter believed that the gang would brand him a failure if he did not follow through and a hero if he did. They stroked his ego when he flashed a gun, and then they pointed out whom to shoot.

Collusion among the shooter, his prime supporter, and other gang members also was evident in the other two cases. The relationships among key gang members placed the shooters in action roles, whereas the drivers and other passengers took passive roles and simply followed orders.

Group Pressure Group pressure served as another component ᶠ the drive-by shooting scenarios. The shooters either were ᵗed, encouraged, or ordered to shoot. The group expected the shooters to take action, and the shooters, in all cases, expected to gain support for their behavior. This anticipation of group support influenced their actions, and what started as idle talk among gang members led to violent confrontations. As the incidents unfolded, a group sense of willingness to find trouble also emerged as infectious agitation and excitement spread throughout the group.

Availability of Weapons The introduction of a gun served as a catalyst in moving each incident to violence. As the ultimate source of power, the gun provided excitement and gave the shooter a quick route to stature. It was an instrument used to impress others in the gang and the community with the group's ability to act in battle.

Ancillary Confrontations The drive-by shootings studied were not isolated events. They occurred as one in a series of crimes. In one case, the confrontation that preceded the shooting was a continuation of a vendetta against minorities. In the others, shootings were a prelude to, or a continuation of, other acts of violence.

Stages in the Shooting Events

News reporters and academicians often associate gang violence with competition over turf or drug markets. The shootings examined here were not about drugs or gang territory. They were about guns, excitement, and an enhanced reputation.

The studied shootings started with idle gang members looking for trouble. Several confrontations occurred before shots were fired. Those confrontations generated a commitment to action that culminated in drive-by shootings.

Looking for Trouble All of the gang members involved were drunk or associated with a gathering where alcohol was consumed in large amounts. One participant reported using other drugs as well. Gang members sought action; they dressed for battle and had weapons available. They interpreted glances from potential adversaries as invitations to do battle. In one case, two of the four participants did not even witness the initial encounter; yet, they felt compelled to take action later.

The Affront Gang members did not plan the initial encounters. Rather, the incidents evolved as spontaneous reactions to the presence of perceived adversaries—people of a different race and/or people who appeared to identify with a different gang. In all cases, taunts directed at the intended victims characterized the first confrontations.

Interestingly, the initial encounters found the eventual aggressors at a disadvantage because they had not yet decided how to react. Retaliation for failure to show deference to the gang required a group consensus that came later. In two of the cases studied, weapons subsequently used in the drive-by shootin were not readily available during the initial confrontations.

Commitment to Action In each case studied, the shooters returned to the scene of the affront only after a period of consensus building and a group decision to act. The commitment phase generated more excitement—a key motivator for action—and served as the staging point needed to bring the actual event to fruition. The participants described feeling intense excitement en route to the shooting. In all cases, other gang members encouraged the shooters to fire.

The Shooting Each of the above-mentioned factors combined to produce the drive-by shootings. Distinct roles emerged from the incidents. Two of the shooters had held structurally weak positions in the gang and committed the shootings in an attempt to bolster their stature within the group. One shooter sought to maintain his role as a powerful gang member by doing the shooting. All acted to impress others.

The shooting episodes generated their own momentum to produce violent outcomes. The participants' individual histories, their unique roles within the gangs, their need for esteem, and their desire to hurt others in order to feel good about themselves influenced the development of the shootings. Group pressure and heightened levels of excitement moved the gang to violence.

The Aftermath Following the shootings, two typical results emerged—boasting and worrying. In one case, gang members, elated after murdering their victim, bragged to a couple of girls and later displayed news clippings of the incident. Another shooter's boasting continued even in jail, and he viewed time in jail as an opportunity to bolster his image further. He bragged of his status as a killer of rivals, wrote gang graffiti on his jail cell wall, and found the experience to be an enhancement, not a detriment, to his status. The shooter in the third incident tried to brag, but other participants, overcome by fear, discouraged him.

Gang members had not considered the consequences of their actions or worried about the outcome until after the fact—either as soon as the shooting took place or not until the police investigation focused on them. Even the threat of jail did not serve as an effective deterrent. Blind to the consequences, no one thought of getting caught until after the shootings. . . .

The Nature of Gangs

Gang members link their identity to the group, which constantly reinforces their rebel image. Most gang members tend to have fragile egos and turn to violence as a way to gain status within the gang and to stroke their egos. They often view violence as rewarding because it is a means to impress others in an exciting and deviant way, which carries influence with the gang. Drive-by shootings, therefore, can be an exciting and violent

141

path to higher rank within the gang.

Because gang members believe violent behavior will be rewarded, they tend to rationalize their actions. If they fail to weigh the consequences, which is usually the case, other behavioral controls, such as past values learned or threats of punishment, cannot halt the aggression.

In fact, gangs lure others into joining by providing social and material benefits. They offer an exciting lifestyle that prepares members to commit crimes.

Excitement, identity, power, and the influence of friends are key factors leading to violence. The excitement and group pressure associated with drive-by shootings override the factors that might otherwise discourage gang members from committing violent acts. . . .

Be Aware

Among the cases in this study, no key individual drove the gang to violence. Rather, the interaction of a leader, an agitator, and other gang members precipitated the shootings. This observation suggests that less effort should be expended in identifying a leader so as to apply the guillotine theory of suppression. This tactic assumes that eliminating the leader will cause the violent group to fold, which was proven not to be the case. Instead, law enforcement should analyze potentially violent coalitions among key members and focus on dissolving the entire collusive network.

In addition, communities need to be aware of youth gangs cruising for trouble. Gatherings of drunken youths preceded each shooting in this study. Youths assembled in alleys, homes, and parking lots and then went looking for action. Residents were aware of the presence of troublemakers but did nothing. Citizen awareness and a timely police and community response might have prevented violence by defusing the agitation. An action plan may include an effort to monitor automobile and foot traffic within selected neighborhoods and to deal with the "dangerous traffic," i.e., gang youths who appear to be searching aimlessly for excitement.

Some community residents report that the sounds of gunshots form a normal part of neighborhood life. In this study, the introduction of a weapon into the hands of volatile and irresponsible youths had enormous consequences. The weapon was both a powerful influence and a novelty. It became a focus of attention and a tool to achieve status. . . .

The Causes of Violence

Although the drive-by shooting participants studied here belonged to gangs, the influence of the gang organization, as whole, on the shooting was subtle. This observation suggests that gang conflicts may be less of a problem than anticipated in causing some drive-by shootings. In the study, the elements that led to violence included identification with a gang, but a history of criminality, a background of alcohol and substance abuse, and the quest for excitement and esteem held equal importance. . . .

Contrary to the researcher's expectations, the study revealed that organized gang activities, such as drug and turf wars, did not have a strong relationship to the drive-by shootings studied. Rather, gang members viewed such shootings as a means to provide excitement and to improve their status within the gang's hierarchy.

The shooters in the cases examined were young people seeking excitement and trying to build a reputation. The victims died from a lethal combination of the shooters' thoughtless reaction to provocation, the encouragement of the group, and the presence of a gun.

"Kids really want to be disciplined. . . . They get discipline from the gang they don't get at home."

A Need for Discipline Contributes to Gang-Related Crime

Suzanne Fields

Juveniles join gangs to fulfill their need for camaraderie, emotional support, and discipline, syndicated columnist Suzanne Fields argues in the following viewpoint. Fields contends that youths who engage in gang-related crime and violence have not received adequate discipline from their parents or from society. These young people should be given strong punishments, she concludes, in order to help them turn their lives around.

As you read, consider the following questions:

1. What is the symbol of Robert "Yummy" Sandifer's gang, according to Fields? What does she say this symbol represents?
2. How could the lives of "Yummy" and his victim have been saved, in Fields's opinion?

Suzanne Fields, "Virtue Perverted in Gang Violence," *Conservative Chronicle*, September 21, 1994. Reprinted by permission of the author.

Big Johnny was my father's best friend. He was a tall and tough Italian—"the big wop"—who once saved the life of my father—"the little Jew"—in the mean streets of Washington in the 1920s. That's the gritty way they talked about each other back then. Loyalty was the glue of their friendship.

We used to call my dad "The Mighty Midge." He said that little guys needed big guys to depend on.

Most boys learn these lessons from their fathers first and later in friendships of mutual support. That's what middle-class and upper-class fraternities and clubs are all about: comradeship, loyalty, discipline and protection. These clans don't always live up to their own high standards and often descend into an "animal house," or their members become intolerant snobs. But their creeds usually demand adherence to specific virtues.

The Role of Gangs

Similarly, poor boys seek succor from gangs. Such gangs don't have to become violent. In fact, I was struck by the good sense written into the code of the gang to which 11-year-old Robert "Yummy" Sandifer belonged, the Chicago kid who was identified by an eyewitness as the murderer of a 14-year-old girl and who was later slain himself, probably by fellow gang members.

The gang's symbol is a six-pointed star, which represents "love, life and loyalty," which lead to "wisdom, knowledge and understanding." The gang's rules include a taboo on consuming addictive drugs, and all gang members—or "soldiers"—are instructed regardless of rank or position to strive to help each other.

Yummy was a little guy who grew up in a vicious environment, abused and neglected by his mother, a kid who wanted the protection and emotional support of the "big guns" of his gang. He was willing to do anything to get it, including murder. He was a hardened criminal at the usually tender age of 11, on probation for armed robbery, the toughest penalty a child his age could get.

The Value of Discipline

In June 1994, when police caught him in a stolen car, he was sent to a center for juveniles. When the Department of Children and Family Services became acquainted with this difficult and dangerous child, they demanded sterner justice, including long-term imprisonment in another state. But a judge, more concerned with the child's "rights" than the larger rights of his community, refused to keep him in the center for older offenders. Imagine what a bad influence they might be on this child.

"Kids really want to be disciplined," Jeffery Haynes, a youth worker on the South Side of Chicago, told the *Chicago Tribune.* "They get discipline from the gang they don't get at home." He

145

might have added that they get punishment and protection from the gang they don't get from the law.

Psychological interpretations of how a blossoming child turns rotten are easy to find and often include a little truth. Abused children are much more likely to engage in criminal behavior than children who aren't. Children born to single teenage mothers are more likely to have problems than those born to married older women. Yummy's father has been in prison for the last five years. But not all "victimized" children become criminals, and many states are beginning to lock up child criminals regardless of their age or personal history, adhering to the idea that if you do a man's crime you do a man's time.

Reprinted by permission of Mike Thompson and Copley News Service.

If the little guy "Yummy," so nicknamed because he loved cookies, had been put away in prison, he and his 14-year-old victim would probably be alive today.

No amount of moralizing can save the Yummies of the world, and no simple solution can emerge from these horrible murders. But until a cultural revolution takes place in the United States, one that reinforces the child's universal desire for discipline, and that builds on a father's love, we'll continue to count expanding numbers of slum kids without conscience, without a sense of right and wrong.

Big Johnny and my father were no angels in the rough-and-tumble world in which they grew up, but both had a strong sense of right and wrong, of good and bad, if often honored mostly in the breach. They grew old as good friends together, trading stories about "how tough times can make a monkey eat red pepper." They definitely understood the meaning of the ideals of the Chicago gang's six-pointed star: Love, life and loyalty lead to wisdom, knowledge and understanding. But you have to live longer than 11 years to learn it.

"People who aren't familiar with gangs think that these kids should just say no. But in the gang world, saying no can get you killed."

Fear of Violence Contributes to Gang-Related Crime

Jon D. Hull

In the following viewpoint, *Time* news correspondent Jon D. Hull describes the difficulties many young people experience when they attempt to leave their gang. According to Hull, such youths must endure a ritual—called being "violated" or "jumped out"—in which they are severely beaten by members of the gang they are leaving. In addition, he contends, youths who drop out of gang life become vulnerable to attack by former rivals as well as to continued harassment by members of their own former gang. Hull concludes that the fear produced by these various threats keeps many juveniles from escaping involvement in gang-related crime and violence.

As you read, consider the following questions:

1. In Hull's assessment, what is the safest way to leave a gang? Why is this strategy difficult for younger members?
2. According to the author, why do gang members who leave often return to their former gangs?
3. How does Enrique Quiroz say he deals with his conscience over beating friends who decide to get out of his gang, as quoted by the author?

Jon D. Hull, "No Way Out," *Time*, August 17, 1992; ©1992 Time Inc. Reprinted with permission.

With his crazy stare, massive knuckles and tattooed biceps, Jimmy T. looks like an urban grenade with a faulty pin. The five-alarm face fits nicely with his career as an up-and-coming member of a Chicago gang called the Vice Lords. But when his face relaxes and the baby fat sinks back in place, a different visage emerges. Disarmed of weapons and bravado, Jimmy is a terrified 16-year-old who did something very, very stupid one hot summer night this past June.

"O.K., it was like this," he says, rubbing those big hands together and rocking slightly in his chair. "They told me, 'Time to put in some work for your homies. Here's the gun. There's the car. Get up and go, boy.'" In other words, welcome to the big time, Jimmy. Time to prove your stuff by shooting some rivals. Try not to hit someone's mama or baby, but mainly just pull the trigger bang bang bang—and don't lose the damned gun.

Only thing was, Jimmy wanted nothing to do with the big time. Like most kids in his West Side neighborhood, he just sort of fell into gang banging at 14. Then things got crazy, and now he wants out.

A muggy Saturday night shortly after 11. Jimmy is driving around in a stolen 1987 Honda Prelude, a 9-mm TEC-9 under the seat. "I'm thinking, ohhh, man, this s___ ain't for me. I'm just tired of this gang banging, and I'm, like, *real* scared." A semiliterate high school dropout, Jimmy grapples with the ghetto's version of a mid-life crisis. He drives around for 40 minutes, carefully obeying every traffic signal as he furiously works through his options. Definitely don't want to be stopped by the police, really don't want to fire this gun and sure as hell don't want to disappoint the gang. Absolute ground zero in the mind of a gang banger. "I'm thinking it through, and finally it comes to decision time." Jimmy wheels the Honda toward a group of faceless teenagers hanging on a corner in rival turf and blasts seven rounds into the crowd, wounding three.

Days later, he tries to explain why he did it. "Damn, man, don't you know what would happen to me if I just told my gang I want out? That I'm scared?"

You can ask Keith Smith, a minister's son in Waukegan, Ill. Smith called it quits last August after eight months of gang banging with a pack called the Latin Lovers. The de-initiation ceremony took place right before midnight in a local park. The ground rules: four against one for three minutes, no weapons. Smith, then 15, collapsed after the first minute. He remained in a coma for 58 days.

Or ask Thomas R., an 18-year-old former member of a Crip set in Los Angeles who just said no to his fellow gang members ast April. "They did me pretty bad," he says softly. Bad meaning a broken arm, a broken wrist, two teeth knocked out, lots of cigarette burns on his face and a few dozen bruises, which really isn't too bad for the Crips. But Thomas cautions, "You bet they ain't done with me yet."

The quickest exit from gang life is via the morgue. The surest route is a one-way ticket out of the old neighborhood. For most young gang members, that leaves no choice at all. "Just to walk away and get out? God, you may get killed," says Daniel Swope, executive director of a community group called BUILD in Chicago. "You make a commitment, and it's lifelong."

Most young gang bangers don't even think about getting out. The money and security are too good and the alternatives too few. The gang is a surrogate family and the only source of approval, however convoluted, that they'll ever know. Pathetically, all the bloodshed is merely a by-product of an utterly misguided and frantic inner-city search for respect. "What other world do these kids know?" asks George Knox, director of the Gang Crime Research Center at Chicago State University.

But some guys do get wise. Something about all the guns and death and arrests just adds up. "I was scared I'd have to shoot somebody," says Juan Vanga, 22, who took a three-minute beating from five guys to get out of the Latin Kings in Chicago last year. "Hell, five of my friends are already dead." Some guys get bored. "I wasn't scared or anything," says Eddie Calderon, 16, who quit the Latin Kings last month in a flurry of blows. "I just got sick and tired of holding the guns."

The safest way out of a gang—short of fleeing—is to fade away very carefully. This is more plausible for members 19 and older, who have paid their dues and can now use jobs, wives or children as excuses for not hanging out with the homeboys. But most younger gang members have nowhere to fade away to. Meanwhile, gang bangers are notorious for overreacting at the smallest perceived slight. "You got to earn your respect," says Salvador Nevarez, 23, who joined the Disciples at 13 but married two years ago and now works as a salesman for Montgomery Ward in Chicago. "There is no such thing as ever getting out. You just drift away." Nevarez is well into his ninth life. "I had a lot of shoot-outs, but I never got shot," he says appreciatively. His advice to the younger guys? "Only way for a young guy to get out is to get killed."

Even the military, once an honorable way out of the 'hood, has gradually closed its doors to all but the most qualified applicants, which usually excludes gang members. "There are a hell of a lot of gang members that would like to get out," says Sergeant Wes McBride of the Los Angeles County sheriff's department. "But there are not a lot of social programs out there to help them." For a 14-year-old living in a housing project run by a gang, it doesn't cut it to plead a hectic schedule when the guys come knocking

"If you're in the projects, getting out of a gang just isn't a sm~
thing to do," says J.W. Hughes, 22, a former member of a ga~
called the Black Disciples in Chicago who now counsels ga~
members. "You have to fear for your life." BUILD's Swope wa~
"If you don't show up for meetings, they issue a B.O.S. [bea~
sight] order." Or worse.

Those who dare "drop the flag" and resign from the gang
a brutal little ceremony called being "violated" or "jumped out."
The precise ritual varies from gang to gang: sometimes each
member of the gang, which may be several dozen strong, gets a
free swing at the victim; other times four or five members are
assigned to conduct the beating for a set amount of time. Whatever the punishment, the results are strikingly similar. "They
give you a head-to-toe, which means you get your ass kicked,"
says Frank Perez, program director for the Chicago Commons
Association gang project.

The Best Option

Our major mistake is to assume that inner-city youth are clamor-
ing to join gangs. In reality, even in gang-infested neighborhoods
many youth steer clear of them. The rest often join because membership represents the best option out of a miserable few choices.

Malcolm W. Klein, *Los Angeles Times*, September 29, 1995.

Eddie Hernandez, 22, formerly of the Disciples on Chicago's
Southwest Side, recalls the first time he ever saw a guy being
jumped out. "They made this guy walk through an alley filled
with gang members," he says. "Aw, man, it was awful. That guy
was unconscious after just a few feet." Hernandez doesn't shy
from violence easily. In his seven-year career, he's been shot in
the stomach, hit in the head with a railroad tie, had his arm broken in a fight, absorbed countless punches, and been jailed twice
for auto theft—not to mention all the unspeakable things he's
done to other people. Last May he told his fellow gang members
he had finally had enough. His former friends promptly jumped
and beat him, stabbing him in the hand during a knife fight. "If
they see me by myself, I'll be jumped again," he says matter-of-
factly.

Perez counsels teenagers to go public with their desire to quit a
gang only as a last resort. "It beats getting killed or blowing
somebody's brains out," he explains. Most antigang workers are
adamantly against such advice under any conditions. "That
would be like telling the kid to go kill himself," says Swope. Then

there are folks like Marianne Diaz-Parton, a gang-intervention worker for the Community Youth Gang Services Project in Los Angeles, who actually condone the beatings.

Diaz-Parton, 33, joined Los Compadres at 13 and served three years in prison for shooting two rival gang members with a sawed-off shotgun. Since "retiring," she is frequently asked by frightened female gang members trying to get out of gangs to monitor their beatings. "They know I've got juice with the gangs," she says with considerable pride. She recalls the case of Priscilla, a 15-year-old who wanted out. Three other girls, all gang bangers, took Priscilla into a public rest room while Diaz-Parton waited outside to make sure things didn't get too out of hand. "They went at her for three minutes. You could hear it, all right," she says. Fearing legal complications, Diaz-Parton stopped accepting such invitations three years ago but argues, "Society looks at being jumped out as something barbaric. To me it's not out of line. Hey, if you're in a fraternity, don't they mess with you? Only with gangs they take it a step further. That way you leave with dignity."

Fat chance. Even those who endure a beating are not spared future harassment. And getting out means losing the protection of your gang while retaining all your old enemies, who don't stop to ask questions. Those who do manage to escape their gang while remaining in the neighborhood are often sucked back in by a confluence of raw fear and sheer necessity. "The pressure is just too damn strong," concedes Commander Robert Dart, who heads the Chicago police department's gang unit. "You can't be an island out there."

Many anxious inner-city parents send their children to live with relatives out of state. Unfortunately, many of these kids simply start new gangs, rather than new lives, in Grandma's neighborhood. "They've just transported the cancer," says Sergeant McBride, who has a large map on his office wall covered with red and blue flags showing how the Los Angeles Crips and Bloods have metastasized across the country.

Police in Wichita (pop. 300,000) arrested their first transplanted L.A. gang members in 1989. Now Sedgwick County, which includes Wichita, is riddled with 68 different gang sets boasting 1,400 members. Last August, Reginaldo Cruz, 15, was taken to a park, forced to his knees and fatally shot in the head and chest with a .410-gauge shotgun. Though the suspect remains at large, police believe Cruz was executed for trying to get out of a gang called the Vato Loco Boyz. Says Kent Bauman, an officer with the city's gang-intelligence unit: "People who aren't familiar with gangs think that these kids should just say no. But in the gang world, saying no can get you killed."

Local residents seized on a creative response early one morning last May, when members of Pastor Chuck Chipman's congregation descended on a gang-infested neighborhood to rescue a 12-year-old boy being forced to work as a drug courier for a gang that was threatening him and his family. Before gang members could react, the entire family of four and all its belongings were whisked away to a safe house.

That evacuation prompted a local group called Project Freedom to construct a network dubbed the underground railroad to funnel gang members and their families to safety in cases where all else fails. Six former gang members and two families have been shuttled to safety through a patchwork of churches both in and out of the state. The relocations are coordinated with the Wichita police, who check for outstanding warrants. Project Freedom pays for the initial move, while local congregations agree to assume housing costs and arrange for jobs and education for as long as two years. "It's a stopgap measure," concedes executive director James Copple, who tours the city's rougher neighborhoods on weekend nights wearing a bulletproof vest. "If we have to relocate them, then in some ways we've already lost the battle."

An underground railroad may be impractical, but so are most of the other options available to a young gang banger who wants out. At least Project Freedom is saving lives. Frances Sandoval, founder of Mothers Against Gangs in Chicago, gets tearful phone calls from parents with kids too scared to leave a gang but terrified of staying in. "Unfortunately, there is very little I can offer them," she says. "In most cases it's hopeless unless they can literally pack up and leave. And we're talking about moving to another state."

Surprisingly, even many loyal gang members admit that their ranks would be thinned if quitting wasn't so dangerous. "People want to get out of gangs, but they're afraid of getting whooped," says Enrique Quiroz, 20, a hard-core member of the Latin Kings in Chicago. Quiroz, a lumbering fellow who has been shot at 12 times, jailed five times, sliced in the elbow and the chin and had his hands broken with a bat, is exactly the kind of guy who makes getting out so problematic. Although he acknowledges some qualms about cracking the heads of close friends who want out of the gang, he has a simple technique for dealing with his conscience. "I've never done it sober," he admits sheepishly. "Only time I do it is when I'm high or drunk and you know you just get going with the guys and get yourself really worked up."

Then it's all flying fists and boots and maybe even a knife or chain until the rage is exhausted and a body drops to the ground—just another punk expelled from the pack.

153

Periodical Bibliography

The following articles have been selected to supplement the diverse views presented in this chapter. Addresses are provided for periodicals not indexed in the *Readers' Guide to Periodical Literature*, the *Alternative Press Index*, or the *Social Sciences Index*.

Robert Coles — "Gang Members: Their Street Education," *New Oxford Review*, June 1994. Available from 1069 Kains Ave., Berkeley, CA 94706.

Aaron Collins — "Gangbanger," *Angolite*, September/October 1993. Available from Louisiana State Penitentiary, Angola, LA 70712.

Mike Davis — "In L.A., Burning All Illusions," *Nation*, June 1, 1992.

Vanessa Fuhrmans — "Youth Gangs Hit the Small Time," *Governing*, May 1992.

William Grigg — "America's New 'Urban Leaders,'" *New American*, April 4, 1994. Available from 770 Westhill Blvd., Appleton, WI 54914.

Camille Harper — "Do the Wrong Thing," *Women's Quarterly*, Summer 1995. Available from 2111 Wilson Blvd., Suite 550, Arlington, VA 22201-3057.

Harper's Magazine — "Family Values: The Gangster Version," April 1995.

Stuart H. Isett — "From Killing Fields to Mean Streets," *World Press Review*, December 1994.

Salim Muwakkil — "Ganging Together," *In These Times*, April 5–18, 1993.

Seth Mydans — "Gangs Reach a New Frontier: Reservations," *New York Times*, March 18, 1995.

Clarence Page — "Taking the Glamour Out of Gang Life," *Liberal Opinion Week*, August 24, 1992. Available from 108 E. Fifth St., Vinton, IA 52349.

Matthew Purdy — "Using the Racketeering Law to Bring Down Street Gangs," *New York Times*, October 19, 1994.

Luis J. Rodriguez — "Turning Youth Gangs Around," *Nation*, November 21, 1994.

4 CHAPTER

How Can Juvenile Crime Be Combated?

Juvenile
Crime

Chapter Preface

In response to increasing public concern about the problem of juvenile crime, law enforcement officials, politicians, and citizens have advocated various measures designed to prevent delinquency. Attempted solutions include midnight basketball programs, transferring violent youths to adult courts, and sending juvenile offenders to military-style boot camps. One response that has gained a great deal of popularity in many cities is the enforcement of curfew ordinances.

Public officials and others advocate curfew regulations as a means of keeping teenagers off the streets and out of trouble. Such laws have been on the books in many U.S. cities for decades, although they have largely gone unenforced. In recent years, existing curfew ordinances have been revived and new ones have been created. These laws generally require youths under eighteen to be off the streets by 11 P.M. on weekdays and by midnight on weekends. Violators are picked up by police and released into their parents' custody. In some cities, the parents of repeat offenders can be subjected to fines.

Many commentators, however, argue that curfews are ineffective. James Fox, a criminologist at Northeastern University, maintains that most juvenile crime takes place between 3 P.M. and 8 P.M., so an 11 P.M. curfew is likely to have little impact. Other critics contend that curfew laws violate the constitutional rights of young people. The American Civil Liberties Union, which is actively challenging city curfew ordinances in courts nationwide, argues that the regulations infringe on teenagers' "fundamental freedoms of speech, assembly, and the right to travel."

Curfew supporters defend the constitutionality of the laws. They point out that the rights of minors can legally be regulated to a greater degree than the rights of adults. Some courts have also ruled that the goals of reducing juvenile crime and promoting public safety justify the imposition of limits on young people's freedoms. In upholding a curfew law in Dallas, the U.S. Court of Appeals for the Fifth Circuit stated, "It is true that the curfew ordinance would restrict some late-night activities of juveniles. . . . But when balanced with the compelling interest sought to be addressed—protecting juveniles and preventing juvenile crime—the impositions are minor."

The debate over the constitutionality of curfews reveals how difficult it can be to balance the rights of individual citizens against society's interest in maintaining public safety. The use of curfews is among the issues debated in the following chapter on measures to combat juvenile crime.

"We must remain deadly serious about targeting . . . juvenile criminals for arrest, prosecution, and incarceration."

Law Enforcement Can Effectively Combat Juvenile Crime

John J. DiIulio Jr.

In the following viewpoint, John J. DiIulio Jr. argues that tough law enforcement policies have reduced crime rates in many American cities. He contends that such efforts are a necessary response to the threat posed by a growing population of teenage males, which he says will subject America to a wave of violent crime in the near future. Among other recommendations, DiIulio favors prosecuting and incarcerating dangerous juvenile criminals as adults. DiIulio, a professor of politics and public affairs at Princeton University, is director of the Center for Public Management at the Brookings Institution, a public policy research organization.

As you read, consider the following questions:

1. By what percentage did juvenile arrests decrease in Jacksonville, Florida, between 1993 and 1994, according to DiIulio?
2. According to the author, how many more young criminals will be on the streets in 2000?
3. What three interlocking anti-crime strategies does DiIulio propose?

Serious crime is declining in many big cities across America. That's the good news. Meanwhile, the country's largest and most violent cohort of young males will soon reach its crime-prone years. That's the bad news. But demography is not fate. Smarter law enforcement and tougher sentencing policies explain much of the recent drop in crime, and can minimize the damage from the next crime wave.

Dropping Crime Rates

Between 1993 and 1994, the violent crime rate declined by 10 percent or more in eight of the 10 cities with the highest violent-crime rates (Miami, New York City, Los Angeles, Tallahassee, Baton Rouge, Little Rock, Jacksonville, and Pueblo, Colorado). In many cities, a sizable reduction in homicides accounts for much of the fall in these rates. For example, the number of murders in Atlanta, Chicago, and New Orleans together plummeted by 17 percent during the first half of 1995 compared with the same period in 1994.

New York City and Houston have enjoyed truly phenomenal drops in serious crimes, including murder. In 1992 and again in 1993, more than 1,900 homicides were committed in the Big Apple. But in 1994 New York City's murder count fell to 1,581. Through July 1995, it suffered fewer than 700 murders, and it continued to show declines of 10 percent or more in robberies, burglaries, and most other serious crimes. Likewise, the number of people murdered in Houston declined by 32 percent during the first half of 1995 compared with the same period in 1994. Rapes in Houston decreased by 21 percent, robberies by 15 percent, and the overall violent crime rate by 7 percent.

While New York City and Houston are leading the pack, other cities are catching up. During the first half of 1995, for example, the overall crime rate was down by more than 16 percent in San Francisco, 10 percent in San Antonio, and 6 percent in both Los Angeles and Philadelphia. And the number of murders declined by more than 6 percent in Philadelphia and Los Angeles, 9 percent in Detroit, and 10 percent in Boston and St. Louis.

What is going on here? Some criminologists dismiss the recent improvement in the crime rate as a mere statistical fluke. But it is hard to imagine that these downward trends, occurring in consecutive years in given jurisdictions, could have happened by chance. Others insist that the slide in crime rates is greased by a dwindling population of teenage boys. There is something to this claim, but it ignores the inconvenient fact that Houston and some other places with growing populations of at-risk youth have nonetheless experienced sharp reductions in crime.

Finally, a few criminologists have rushed to relate the dive in crime rates to everything from a sudden surge in the efficacy of gun control laws (which is patently absurd) to changes in the patterns of drug use (for example, the decline in crack-cocaine use which, they insist, has had nothing to do with anti-drug law enforcement). One much-quoted criminologist has even declared, "What goes up must come down."

Enforcement Counts

In many cities, the decline in crime rates can be explained at least in part by law-enforcement efforts that capitalize on community crime-fighting initiatives and take bad guys off the streets. I call this explanation Bratton's Law in honor of New York City's police commissioner, William Bratton. Like most veteran professionals in the justice system, Bratton understands perfectly well that crime rates are not determined solely by what cops, courts, and corrections agencies do. But his impatience with criminological cant about the inefficacy of policing practices and sentencing policies on crime rates is both ennobling and enlightening. Three brief examples illustrate Bratton's Law in action.

Jacksonville. In July 1991, Harry L. Shorenstein became state attorney for the Fourth Judicial Circuit in Jacksonville, Florida. At that time Jacksonville was besieged by violent crime, much of it committed by juvenile offenders. In the year before Shorenstein arrived, juvenile arrests had risen by 27 percent, but most young habitual criminals were released quickly. Jacksonville's finest were doing their best to remove serious young criminals from the streets, but the rest of the system was not following suit.

Then, in March 1992, Shorenstein instituted an unprecedented program to prosecute and incarcerate dangerous juvenile offenders as adults. In most parts of the country, juvenile criminals for whom the law mandates adult treatment are not actually eligible for state prison sentences and are routinely placed on probation without serving any jail time. But Shorenstein's program was for real. He assigned 10 veteran attorneys to a new juvenile-prosecutions unit. Another attorney, funded by the Jacksonville Sheriffs Office, was assigned to prosecute repeat juvenile auto thieves.

By the end of 1994, the program had sent hundreds of juvenile offenders to Jacksonville's jails and scores more to serve a year or more in Florida's prisons. Jacksonville's would-be juvenile street predators got the message, and the effect of deterrence soon appeared in the arrest statistics. From 1992 to 1994, total arrests of juveniles dropped from 7,184 to 5,475. From 1993 to 1994, juvenile arrests increased nationwide and by over 20 percent in Florida. But Jacksonville had a 30 percent decrease in all juvenile arrests, including a 41 percent decrease in juveniles arrested for weapons offenses, a 45 percent decrease for auto

159

theft, and a 50 percent decrease for residential burglary. Although Jacksonville still has a serious violent crime problem, the number of people murdered there during the first half of 1995 declined by 25 percent compared with the same period in 1994.

Houston. Almost a thousand officers have been added to the city's police force since 1991. Led by Police Chief Sam Nuchia, Houston has a cost-effective police overtime program that puts more cops on the street when and where they are most needed. Residents of Washington, D.C., which fields the highest number of police officers per capita of any major city, know that more police manpower does not necessarily produce less crime or better police performance. But in Houston, Nuchia has used the additional manpower to jump-start community anti-crime activities.

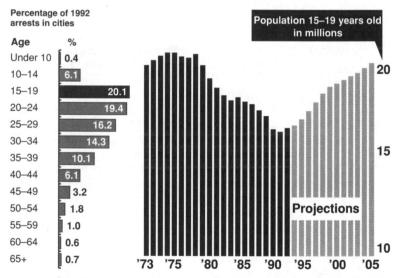

The Coming Youth Crime Bomb

Percentage of 1992 arrests in cities

Population 15–19 years old in millions

Age	%
Under 10	0.4
10–14	6.1
15–19	20.1
20–24	19.4
25–29	16.2
30–34	14.3
35–39	10.1
40–44	6.1
45–49	3.2
50–54	1.8
55–59	1.0
60–64	0.6
65+	0.7

Projections

'73 '75 '80 '85 '90 '95 '00 '05

Sources: Federal Bureau of Investigation (arrests); Census Bureau (population); *New York Times* (graphic).

To cite just one example, Houston's Citizen Patrol Program has operated in more than a hundred of the city's neighborhoods. Among other things, thousands of citizen patrollers have observed and reported suspicious or criminal behavior, from assaults to narcotics dealing to vandalism. Many once-troubled neighborhoods have gone as long as three consecutive months without needing to call for police service. Indeed, two studies found that Nuchia's enforcement efforts not only contributed to

160

Houston's falling crime rates, but also improved police emergency response times, raised police productivity, and reduced citizens' fear of crime.

New York City. Like Houston, New York City has greatly expanded its police force. Since 1990, the NYPD has grown by 7,000 officers. Under Bratton, police have been directed to crack down on public drinking, graffiti, vandalism, and other public disorders. The NYPD has beefed up action against street gangs and drug traffickers, returned to a policy of frisking suspects for guns and other weapons, and redoubled precinct-level efforts on a wide range of community-policing projects.

In the process, Bratton has promoted a new breed of precinct commanders and made them responsible for finding innovative, cost-effective ways of serving citizens and cutting crime in their neighborhoods. Despite recent corruption scandals, the precinct-based management system is working, NYPD morale is high, and New Yorkers are getting results that range from fewer aggressive panhandlers to fewer shootings and murders.

Academic Ideology

Why, then, are many criminologists so unwilling to admit that law enforcement can cut crime? Part of the answer is that more than a dozen major empirical studies over the last two decades have failed to demonstrate either that police manpower and crime rates vary inversely or that particular types of community-oriented policing practices prevent crime. The most famous of these studies is the Kansas City, Missouri, "preventive-patrol" experiment.

For a year in the early 1970s, Kansas City was divided into three areas, each of which received a different level of auto patrol. The 1974 report on the experiment found that criminal activity, reported crime, rates of victimization (as measured in a follow-up survey), citizen fear, and satisfaction with the police were about the same in all three areas. Active auto patrol—beats where cars cruised the streets conspicuously two to three times more frequently than in the control areas—made no difference at all.

But academic experts who treat such negative findings as the final words on the subject are badly mistaken. George L. Kelling of Northeastern University, the father of the Kansas City research and many other major studies, recently cautioned his colleagues that "generalizing from a study about a specific tactic to other tactics or uses of police is inappropriate." As Kelling observed, "random preventive patrol by automobile for the purpose of creating a feeling of police omnipresence" is a relic of "mid-century policing tactics."

Kelling has scolded those "academic ideologists" in criminology who "do not let research interfere with their conclusions." He keenly characterizes as defeatist dogma their views that "crime stems from basic structural features of society, and until problems like homelessness, social injustice, economic inequalities, and racism are addressed, police impact on crime will be negligible."

As a matter of ideology, denying that law enforcement counts in cutting crime may be trendy, but the policy science of the subject remains far from settled. Following an exhaustive review of the empirical literature on policing, David H. Bayley of SUNY-Albany recently concluded that there has never been "a rigorous, clear-cut test of the association between the visible presence of the police and crime rates." Bayley is now in the early stages of a quasi-experimental study designed to test this relationship while controlling for demographic and other variables related to the incidence of crime. Such fine-tuned research on patrol presence, policing strategies, crime rates, and other key variables has become possible only in the past few years with the development of computer-assisted information systems for police dispatching and management.

Bayley's cutting-edge research will help to identify the general conditions under which tactics and increases in police manpower can curb public disorders and cut crime. For now, there is no solid evidence to dismiss, and every practical reason to uphold, Bratton's Law.

Prison Works

By the same token, there is tremendous empirical support for another proposition that many criminologists reflexively reject: Sentencing policies that keep violent and repeat criminals behind bars contribute mightily to reductions in crime.

I call this proposition Wattenberg's Law in honor of Ben Wattenberg, a scholar at the American Enterprise Institute and a nationally syndicated columnist. As Wattenberg has quipped, "A thug in prison can't shoot your sister." Whatever else incarceration buys us in the way of criminal deterrence, rehabilitation, or retribution, it most definitely pays dividends by preventing crimes that prisoners would commit if they were free.

The U.S. Bureau of Justice Statistics has reported that fully 94 percent of state prisoners have committed one or more violent crimes or served a previous sentence in jail or on probation. Between 1980 and 1993, violent offenders were the greatest contributors to state prison population growth.

Even so, today more convicted violent offenders are serving time on probation and parole than in prison. About a third of all violent crime arrestees are on probation, parole, or pretrial release at the time of their arrest. Recent studies by me and others estimate that most prisoners commit between 12 and 21 serious crimes a year when on the loose.

From 1980 to 1992, the aggregate violent-crime rate in the 10 states where incarceration climbed the most decreased by 8 percent. In the 10 states with the lowest increases in incarceration, violent crime soared, in aggregate, 51 percent. A study published in *Science* calculated that in 1989 alone, the increased use of imprisonment spared Americans an estimated 66,000 rapes, 323,000 robberies, 380,000 assaults, and 3.3 million burglaries. In a research report targeted against California's three-strikes law (life without parole for thrice-convicted felons), the RAND Corp. conservatively estimated that the measure would spare Californians about 340,000 serious crimes a year.

Nationally, state prisoners convicted of violent crimes who were released in 1988 had served an average of only 43 percent of their sentences in confinement. Violent convicts released in 1992 had served an average of 48 percent of their time behind bars. And violent offenders released from state prisons in 1995 served, on average, 50 to 52 percent of their time in confinement. This slow but steady increase in incarceration is the result of a nationwide trend toward tougher sentencing policies, and has already spared millions of Americans from serious crimes.

It is not yet possible to calculate precisely how much tougher incarceration policies have contributed to falling crime rates in particular cities. But in explaining New York City's falling crime rate, consider the fact that roughly half of New York's state prison population, and an even larger fraction of its violent offender population, comes from New York City. Over the last decade, the Empire State's prison rolls have more than doubled, and the amount of time served behind bars by violent and repeat criminals has increased by as much as 50 percent.

A Demographic Crime Bomb

Apparently, it takes a Ph.D. in criminology to doubt that keeping dangerous criminals incarcerated cuts crime and to wonder whether releasing any significant fraction of the nation's 1 million prisoners tonight would result in more serious crime tomorrow.

But criminologists are right about one thing: Americans are sitting on a demographic crime bomb. Most predatory street crimes are committed by men under 25. Today [1995] there are about 7.5 million males aged 14 to 17. By the year 2000, we will have an additional 500,000. About 6 percent of young males are responsible for half the serious crimes committed by their age group. Thus, in 2000 we can expect at least 30,000 more young murderers, rapists, and muggers on the streets than we have today. Worse, since the 1950s each generational cohort of young male criminals has committed about three times more crime

163

than the one before. Despite the recent decline in murder rates, homicides committed by 14- to 17-year-olds between 1985 and 1993 increased by 165 percent (more for minority males). The next wave of homicidal and near-homicidal violence among urban youth is bound to reach adjacent neighborhoods, inner-ring suburbs, and even the rural heartland.

This crime bomb probably cannot be defused. The large population of seven- to 10-year-old boys now growing up fatherless, Godless, and jobless—and surrounded by deviant, delinquent, and criminal adults—will give rise to a new and more vicious group of predatory street criminals than the nation has ever known. We must therefore be prepared to contain the explosion's force and limit its damage.

While there is some room for reasonable disagreements about policy tactics—for example, whether the federal role in crime control should be expanded, or whether we should invest more in drug treatment or drug interdiction—any effective anti-crime policy must advance one or more of three interlocking anti-crime strategies: hardening targets, targeting the hardened, and targeting resources.

Hardening the Target

Over the last decade or so, most Americans have taken steps to make the places where they live, work, go to school, or recreate impervious to crime. People have moved out of high-crime neighborhoods, installed antiburglary devices, made crime-sensitive investment decisions, and lectured their children to be mindful of dangers. Businesses and the 32 million Americans who now live in privately governed residential communities have erected security gates and employed more than a million private security guards.

Neighborhoods of every socioeconomic description have formed "town watch" associations and citizen patrol groups. And the poorest of the inner-city poor have battled the ACLU [American Civil Liberties Union] for the right to target-harden their homes, schools, and parks: They erect concrete barriers on streets frequented by drug dealers and prostitutes, evict convicted street thugs from public housing, install metal detectors, and institute random locker searches in public high schools, and more.

Though to a degree hard to quantify, such initiatives have contributed to recent decreases in crime rates and, over time, insulated us somewhat from the failures of our system of justice. But as the next crime wave approaches, we may well be nearing the limit of what private target-hardening measures can do to foster public safety.

Government at all levels, therefore, should do whatever can be done to bolster these protective measures. To offer just two of many possible examples, urban zoning decisions should begin to take into account the criminal consequences of permitting liquor outlets to be so heavily concentrated in high-crime, inner-city neighborhoods. Likewise, urban enterprise zones make sense as ways of giving *de facto* tax credits to businesses willing to locate in high-crime places.

Targeting the Hardened

At the same time, we must redouble our efforts to keep violent and repeat criminals behind bars. To consolidate and expand recent gains, we must be vigilant not only in pushing for truth-in-sentencing and three-strikes measures, but seeing to it that these laws are followed both in letter and in spirit.

Make no mistake: The counter-offensive against tougher sentencing policies is well underway. Aided and abetted by activist federal judges, prisoners' rights activists, journalists, and academic "experts," efforts are already being made to depict these laws as failures and to deny or disparage any suggestion that they have helped account for recent drops in crime rates.

But just ask the criminals. In California, within several months after the three-strikes law went into effect in 1995, an increasing number of parolees began to request inter-state transfers. Likewise, even before Washington State's three-strikes law hit the books in 1993, dozens of sex offenders called the Seattle Police Department with questions about what crimes might count as "strikes." As one career criminal told the detective in charge of the department's sex-offender unit, "It wasn't until [the three-strikes law] passed that I had to say to myself, 'Damn, these people are serious now.'"

As the next crime wave draws near, we must remain deadly serious about targeting hardened adult and juvenile criminals for arrest, prosecution, and incarceration. Anti-incarceration propagandists can be counted on to work overtime with much-publicized tales like the one about the California man whose "third strike" was stealing a slice of pizza from a child in a mall. They failed to note, however, that this criminal had four prior convictions.

Likewise, the anti-incarcerationists are sure to repeat canards about how tougher sentencing policies will bankrupt the country and result in massive prison overcrowding. In truth, we now spend less than half a penny of every tax dollar on prisons, and the costs of prisons can be reduced greatly by cutting back on inmate amenities and services that account for more than half of the prison budget in many states.

As for "overcrowding," despite the growth in the prison population, fewer prisons today are operating over their rated capacity (the number of inmates they were designed to hold) than in

1990. And contrary to popular assertions, there is no systematic empirical evidence to show that double-celling raises the risk of prison disorders, inmate illness, or other serious problems.

Congress is taking steps to target the hardened, as it considers Title III of the Violent Criminal Incarceration Act adopted by the House in February 1995. Known as the Stop Turning Out Prisoners or STOP law, this measure would prohibit activist federal judges from arbitrarily imposing prison caps that result each year in the early release of tens of thousands of dangerous criminals whose return to the streets results in murder and mayhem.

Targeting Resources

Whatever government does henceforth to combat crime should be done in a targeted fashion. It makes no sense, for example, to heed President Clinton's call for spending $8.8 billion in federal dollars for "100,000 cops." As I and many other analysts have proven, not only will that amount not pay for or even seed the funding of anything near 100,000 police officers, but the Justice Department's grant process is rigged to deliver lots of money to small cities that have enough cops and little crime. By the same token, however, it makes even less sense to follow the Republican alternative of dumping more than $10 billion on the states in open-ended anti-crime block grants.

So here is DiIulio's Law: As our euphoria over good news about crime fades and a public panic to "do something" about youth crime begins, let us prepare to honor the overarching conservative principle that government should never spend money it does not have for purposes it has not clearly articulated in order to generate results that cannot easily be evaluated.

"*We approach juvenile crime as a public-health problem, not a law-enforcement problem.*"

Law Enforcement Cannot Effectively Combat Juvenile Crime

Mike Males and Faye Docuyanan

In response to the problem of juvenile crime, many policy makers have advocated tough law-enforcement strategies such as transferring juveniles to adult courts and imposing lengthy prison sentences. In the following viewpoint, Mike Males and Faye Docuyanan argue that these efforts are misguided. They contend that such punitive measures are ineffective and inappropriate because they fail to address the problem of poverty, which the authors believe is the underlying cause of juvenile crime. Males and Docuyanan are social ecology doctoral students at the University of California, Irvine.

As you read, consider the following questions:

1. How do the lengths of sentences of juveniles compare to those of adults in California, according to the authors?
2. According to Gary Taylor, quoted by the authors, what problems exist in the juvenile justice system?
3. How does Wayne Thompson's program reintegrate convicted youths back into their communities, according to Males and Docuyanan?

From Mike Males and Faye Docuyanan, "Crackdown on Kids," *Progressive*, February 1996. Reprinted by permission of the *Progressive*, 409 E. Main St., Madison, WI 53703.

Madness is the word Stephen Bruner uses to describe the summer of 1992. "The things I did, things I had done to me. . . . Madness." It was the summer after eighth grade. He and his gang Panic Zone hung out where the rural black community of Spencer intersects the southeast Oklahoma City suburb of Midwest City. He rattles off the names of a dozen gangs—Hoover Street, Westside, Candlewood, 6-0—that inhabit the district.

For his contribution to the madness, Bruner spent his ninth grade in an Oklahoma juvenile lockup. Now Bruner works as an intern for Wayne Thompson at the Oklahoma Health Care Project in Founder's Tower overlooking the city's opulent northwest side. Thompson himself spent three years in prison in the 1970s at Terminal Island and Lompoc for armed bank robbery on behalf of the San Francisco Black Panther chapter.

Madness, Thompson suggests, is "the natural, predictable reaction" of youths to the "larger, hostile adult culture that is anti-youth, particularly anti-African-American youth."

Twenty thousand more Oklahoma City children and teenagers live in poverty than a quarter of a century ago. "These kids are at risk of extinction if they depend upon adults to protect them," Thompson says. It is not just parents who fail them, but an adult society increasingly angry and punishing toward its youth. "That is the perception of the young people who are being ground up in this culture and the grinder of the juvenile-justice system. Their perception of their situation is very correct."

Harsher Penalties

Today, state after state is imposing harsher penalties on juveniles who run afoul of the law. "The nationwide trend is to get tough on juvenile crime," says Gary Taylor of Legal Aid of Western Oklahoma. Rehabilitation and reintegration into the community are concepts that have already fallen out of fashion for adult criminals. Now they are fast becoming passé for juveniles, as well. Instead of prevention and rehabilitation programs, more prisons are being built to warehouse juveniles along with adults. The trend began in California; it is now sweeping the nation.

Juveniles are being waived into adult court at lower and lower ages. In Wisconsin, ten-year-olds can now be tried as adults for murder. Juveniles convicted of drug offenses in adult court receive lengthy mandatory sentences. In California, studies by the state corrections department show that youths serve sentences 60 percent longer than adults for the same crimes. Oklahoma wants to try thirteen-year-olds as adults and petitioned the Supreme Court to allow executions of fourteen- and fifteen-year-olds.

And it's not just the states. It's the Clinton Administration, too. The *New York Times* reported in December 1995 that "proposals by the Administration would allow more access to juvenile records and give federal prosecutors discretion to charge serious juvenile offenders as adults."

In short, we are giving up on human beings at a younger and younger age.

Poverty Causes Juvenile Crime

Juvenile crime is on the rise. But the reason is not media violence, rap music, or gun availability—easy scapegoats that have little to do with the patterns of violence in real life. Rather, the reason is rising youth poverty.

Sensational press accounts make it seem as though juvenile crime is patternless. It is hardly that. Juvenile crime is closely tied to youth poverty and the growing opportunity gap between wealthier, older people and destitute, younger people. Of California's fifty-eight counties, thirty-one with a total of 2.5 million people recorded zero teenage murders in 1993. Central Los Angeles, which has roughly the same number of people, reported more than 200 teen murders.

In the thirty-one counties free of teenage killers, the same blood-soaked media and rock and rap music are readily available (more, since white suburban families over-subscribe to cable TV), and guns are easy to obtain. Nor can some "innate" teenage qualities be the cause, since by definition those qualities are as present in youths in areas where violent teenage crime is rare as in areas where it is common.

"We see kids from *all* walks of life," says Harry Hartmann, counselor with the L.A. Office of Education. But "the races are skewed to blacks and Hispanics," he acknowledges. Very skewed—six out of seven of those who are arrested for violent juvenile crimes are black or Hispanic. By strange coincidence, that is just about the proportion of the county's youths in poverty who are black or Hispanic.

"Poverty in a society of affluence, in which your self-esteem is tied to failure to achieve that affluence," is a more accurate explanation for our uniquely high level of violence, says Gilbert Geiss, a criminologist formerly with the University of California, Irvine. It's not just "poverty, per se."

Youth Poverty and Crime in L.A.

L.A. County is a clear illustration. Its per-capita income is much higher, and its general poverty rate lower, than the United States as a whole. But its youth poverty rate is staggering: 200,000 impoverished adolescents live in the county.

L.A. County is home to one in fifteen teenage murderers in the United States. Its vast basin harbors such a bewildering array of gangs and posses that estimates of the number of youths allied with them at any one time are almost impossible to pin down.

Jennifer, seventeen, at the Search to Involve Pilipino Americans (SIPA), a local community center, rattles off the names of twenty youth gangs, takes a breath, admits she has left some out. Los Angeles County (population 9 million) has more teen murders than the dozen largest industrial nations outside the United States combined. Of L.A.'s 459 teen murder arrestees in 1994, just twenty-four were white. Blacks and Hispanics predominated, but Asian Americans comprise the fastest-rising group of violent juveniles.

"I tried to ask them, 'Why are you in it?'" Jennifer says. "They don't know. A lot of people regret it after. 'Yeah, that was some stupid shit.' They thought it was so cool." But if stupid, confused kids were the whole problem, why are black kids in Los Angeles a dozen times stupider than white kids? Why are Asians getting stupider faster than anyone else?

As youth poverty rises and becomes more concentrated in destitute urban neighborhoods, violence becomes more concentrated in younger age groups.

But today's reigning criminal-justice experts—UCLA's James Q. Wilson, Northwestern's James Allen Fox, Princeton's John DiIulio, former Robert Kennedy aide Adam Walinsky—dismiss poverty as a cause of youth violence. Instead, they talk about an insidious culture of poverty, and they argue relentlessly that only more cops and more prisons will bring down juvenile crime. Instead of proposing more money for alleviating poverty or for crime prevention, they want more law enforcement—at a cost of tens of billions of dollars.

Writing in the September 1994 *Commentary*, Wilson calls the growing adolescent population "a cloud" that "lurks . . . just beyond the horizon." It will bring "30,000 more muggers, killers, and thieves than we have now." Wilson downplays poverty, racism, poor schools, and unemployment as "not . . . major causes of crime at all." The real problem, he writes, is "wrong behavior" by a fraction of the population (he pegs it at 6 percent) with bad temperament, concentrated in chaotic families and "disorderly neighborhoods."

Justice in the Golden State

If more prisons and surer sentences were the solutions to crime and delinquency, California should be a haven where citizens leave doors unlocked and stroll midnight streets unmenaced. California inaugurated the new era of imprisoning juvenile offenders in Ronald Reagan's second term as governor in 1971, and since then the state has incarcerated a higher percentage of its youths than any other state. By 1993, a state corrections study found teenagers served terms nearly a year longer than adults for equivalent offenses.

170

"I tell parents who want to release their kid to the [juvenile-justice] system: he might come out worse than when he went in," says Gilbert Aruyao of SIPA.

Eleven hundred new state laws passed during the 1980s set longer, more certain prison terms, especially for juveniles. California's forty-one-prison, 140,000-inmate system is the third-largest in the world; only the United States as a whole and China have larger inmate systems.

A Public Health Perspective

The dimensions of the violence problem, especially for young people, have made the case for viewing violence from a public health perspective as well as the criminal justice vantage point. While criminal justice professionals approach violence in terms of investigation, arrest, prosecution, and conviction, public health specialists approach health problems in terms of the interaction between the host, the agent, and the environment.

The *host* is a person whose behavior determines or contributes to a public health problem. Males, especially adolescents and young adults, are at greatest risk for assaultive violence, believing that they need to prove their manhood.

By *environment*, public health specialists mean the broad social, cultural, institutional, and physical forces that contribute to a public health problem. Many translate into an inability by families and communities to transmit positive values to young people, communicate a sense of hope about the future, or teach nonviolent conflict resolution skills.

The public health focus has brought renewed attention to the weaponry of violence: the *agent*. Thus there have been many calls to severely restrict the sales of firearms and, at the very least, to minimize young people's ready access to weapons.

U.S. Department of Justice Office of Justice Programs, *National Institute of Justice Update*, October 1994.

The Golden State's biggest growth industry is corrections. Seven new prisons opened in California from 1989 to 1994, at a cost of $1.3 billion, to accommodate 16,000 more prisoners; today, they confine 28,000 prisoners. From 1995 through 1996, four new prisons, costing $839 million, will open their doors. There's a new prison built every eight months. Each one is full upon opening.

"For that incorrigible 25 percent (of youth offenders), prisons may be the only way to go," says Harry Hartmann of the L.A. Office of Education. "It's really hard for them to change." In California in 1994, 140,000 persons under the age of twenty were arrested for felonies—including one out of five black males, and one in ten Hispanic males ages sixteen through nineteen. If even one-tenth of that number must be imprisoned more or less permanently, the state's minority teenage male population will require four new prisons every year to contain them.

Beyond Race

As youth poverty mushrooms and the attitudes of the larger society become harsher, the traditional markers of race and class are sliding toward new realignments. "There's still a racial element, sure," says Thompson. "But this has gone beyond race now. There's a larger madness."

Says Bruner: "There are white kids in black gangs, blacks in Mexican gangs, Mexicans in white gangs, blacks in white gangs, Asians in black gangs. We don't fight each other that way. It isn't a race thing. It's who's in the 'hood.'"

The *1995 Kids Count Factbook* lists 47,000 impoverished children and adolescents in the Oklahoma City metropolitan area—21,000 whites, 13,500 blacks, 4,500 Native Americans, 3,000 Asian Americans, 5,000 Latinos.

A November 1995 *Daily Oklahoman* series on the metropolis's exploding poverty reported that these adolescents are increasingly isolated, jammed together in a chain of destitute neighborhoods ringing downtown and extending eastward past the suburbs.

"You go to school with them, people ask of this guy you know, 'Is he OK with you, 'cause if he's OK with you, he's OK with me,'" says Bruner. "If you're in a subcultural group, it's no different in society's eyes whether you're in a gang or not. Kids had no choice but to hang with us. Racism is here. You can't run away from it. [But] racism is not just black or white." Nonwhite youths, white youths on the wrong side, "we are all targets."

Bruner is training in office management and in television production and editing through Thompson's program. Enough of his friends remain trapped in the justice system. Bruner sees that as surrender. "They didn't get out like I did; now they're up for murder one."

Bruner says the system is rigged: "I believe they want to keep me and every other black male and minority male and poor kid in the system permanently, send us all to the penitentiary."

In 1988, Oklahoma petitioned the U.S. Supreme Court to execute fourteen- and fifteen-year-olds (and lost only on a 5-4 vote).

"Society wants to kill these kids," says Thompson. "The death penalty. Shooting them in the street. If it can't do that, then killing their spirit."

Gary Taylor, deputy director of Legal Aid of Western Oklahoma, recounts his agency's efforts to reform a juvenile prison system whose brutality and punitive excesses had been exposed nationally. "Beatings, sexual assaults, hog tying, extreme medical punishments, extreme isolation," said Taylor. "It was kid-kid; it was staff-kid."

There was no notion of rehabilitation. San Francisco lawyers for convicted murderer Freddy Lee Taylor investigated his incarceration in the Oklahoma juvenile prison system and found "a concentration-camp environment," attorney Robert Rionda said.

Many of these youths were wrongly imprisoned: they had been removed from their homes because their parents were abusive or neglectful, or the youths had committed minor offenses like curfew violations or truancy. Rionda's firm did not have to look hard to find Freddy Taylor's co-inmates: most were now in state prison serving terms for major felonies.

"There were many, many kids who were in the system because they were poor and in need of supervision, and they turned them into monsters," Rionda said.

In recent years, twice as many Oklahoma youths have been placed in the adult prison system as in the juvenile system. Oklahoma imprisons more of its citizens than any other state except Texas. If forcing youths into the adult prisons and administering harsh punishment is the remedy, Oklahoma, like California, should be a paradise of peace.

Yet arrest figures since the mid-1980s show Oklahoma's juvenile violence growing at twice the already alarming national pace.

A Public-Health Problem

Los Angeles County and Oklahoma City officials stress prevention but note that it is underfunded. The most effective prevention effort by far is to raise fewer children in poverty. However, "reducing child poverty, much less eliminating it, is no longer a paramount priority for either political party," *U.S. News & World Report* pointed out in November 1995.

Wayne Thompson in Oklahoma City takes prevention seriously. "We approach juvenile crime as a public-health problem, not a law-enforcement problem," says Thompson. "Intervene, then trace the pathology back to its source." The source inevitably turns out to be "the low social, educational, and economic status of the families and communities" violent youths come from.

Thompson's program uses employment training and a variety of family services to reintegrate youths who have already been convicted back into their communities. "We want to empower these young people to change the social and economic circumstances of their lives," he says.

An initial evaluation showed that Thompson's program was more effective than law-enforcement approaches in preventing recidivism among delinquent youths as well as preventing younger members of their families from following in their older siblings' footsteps. The clientele served by the program is small—fewer than 100 youths per year.

The adults most responsive to Thompson's approach are in the business community, Republicans more than Democrats, he notes. "That's frightening," he says. "The social services, academia, are bound like serfs to the status quo."

When he talks to Oklahoma City's business groups, Thompson finds growing concern over the costs of more prisons and "alarm in the white community because the gangs are becoming more integrated." He doesn't push charity or altruism.

"I tell them, 'You're going to die in fifteen or twenty years, and you have grandchildren. They're going to have to live with the environment we've created. And we've created a hellacious environment.' This is not just some teenage rite-of-passage problem. The alienation of young people from the traditional institutions is profound. This is the legacy we're leaving: armed camps. If we don't learn how to share with the people who are now powerless, this culture is ultimately going to acquire the means to bring our society to an end."

"Juveniles 14 or older must be tried as adults for violent crimes involving rape, murder, armed robbery, and aggravated assault."

More Juveniles Should Be Tried as Adults

Part I: Gil Garcetti, Part II: Bradley S. O'Leary

In recent years, many states have altered their laws to make it easier to try juveniles as adults. In Part I of the following two-part viewpoint, Los Angeles County district attorney Gil Garcetti advocates this approach. Among other recommendations for reforming the Los Angeles juvenile justice system, he proposes transferring youths accused of the most serious crimes to adult courts. In Part II, Bradley S. O'Leary argues that America's juvenile justice system must emphasize punishment rather than rehabilitation, especially for those youths who have committed violent crimes. He contends that all violent juveniles should be tried in adult courts and should be subject to adult sentences. O'Leary is copublisher of the *O'Leary/Kamber Report*.

As you read, consider the following questions:

1. Who should have the discretion to transfer juveniles to adult court, according to Garcetti?
2. According to O'Leary, what should be the punishment for a child who brings a gun or a knife to school?

Gil Garcetti, "Distinguishing Between Felons and Truants," *Los Angeles Times*, February 7, 1994. Reprinted with permission of the author. Bradley S. O'Leary, "Justice for Young Criminals: Emphasize Punishment," *USA Weekend*, May 13–15, 1994. Copyright 1994, USA TODAY. Reprinted with permission.

I

The juvenile justice system is failing to protect us from the surge in violent crimes committed by young people.

The patchwork of laws put on the books over the past 30 years isn't working. One problem is that the system was designed to help troubled youth who committed minor offenses, but 75% of the current cases in juvenile court are felonies. We need to act immediately to replace it with a coherent program that protects society from violent juvenile criminals, efficiently rehabilitates youths who can be saved—and also knows how to tell the difference.

Core Principles

Here are some principles that could form the core of a revision:

• *Remove many violent offenders from the juvenile system.* Violent youths who are 17 years old should be sent directly to adult court. In 1993, about 50% of the juveniles referred to the Probation Department for possible criminal offenses were 17 years old. So were many juveniles charged with the most serious crimes.

Prosecutors should have discretion to transfer even much younger juveniles accused of the most serious crimes to adult courts. State legislators have proposed lowering the age at which a youth can be tried as an adult from 16 to 14, but the numbers matter less than letting prosecutors use their own judgment. For instance, a 15-year-old is currently in juvenile court [as of February 7, 1994], accused of a double murder. If the murders had occurred nine days later, on his 16th birthday, he could have been tried as an adult and, if convicted, sentenced to life without the possibility of parole. Convicted juvenile offenders must be freed by age 25.

• *Limit juvenile confidentiality.* Society needs to identify juveniles who commit serious crimes and know what happens to them in court. Improvements have been made over the years, but there are still instances where agencies charged with providing services to children are not aware of criminal proceedings involving a child. School officials, for instance, concerned about violating confidentiality laws, have often not told teachers about students who had been convicted of crimes.

• *Deliver real rehabilitation.* Juvenile justice has to efficiently deliver rehabilitative services to juveniles who commit minor offenses. The first step is coordination among all the agencies that assist young people at risk. We need to identify and help the growing number of children who have never had structure or hope in their lives. Government can also offer parents help with parenting skills and intervention before the family structure falls apart.

The present juvenile system puts truants and murderers

176

through the same procedures, including the appointment of attorneys at public expense and long judicial hearings. We need laws that allow better choices between punishment and guidance, and that use resources more wisely.

Accountability

• *Make juveniles—and their parents—accountable.* Punishment that fits the crime must be meted out fairly and with certainty. Currently, juvenile burglars are often sent straight home on probation while adults who commit the same offense get a mandatory prison sentence; this sort of thing makes juvenile offenders believe they can get away with almost anything.

Parents must be held responsible for keeping their children in school. We can enforce violations of the Education Code and at the same time assist parents with "stay in school" programs. Parents must also pay for the damage their children cause, including the cost of graffiti cleanups. Current law provides for restitution of up to $10,000 to victims of juvenile crime. New laws should simplify this recovery and reinforce parental responsibility, while also offering parenting assistance.

REVOLVING DOOR

Henry Payne. Reprinted by special permission of United Features Syndicate.

• *Intervene early to prevent violence later.* This is the most important step we can take to stop juvenile crime. Legislators need to change the laws that prohibit and punish as well as provide programs and funding to give children the skills and motivation to stay in school and away from gangs, drugs and crime.

• *Keep juveniles away from guns.* We must substantially stiffen laws and penalties for juveniles in possession of guns and for adults who make guns available to juveniles. No loopholes, no exceptions.

A new juvenile justice system would quickly reduce the level of fear we all feel. Over the long term, it would reduce the number of juvenile and adult violent criminals. We need to put reformers to work right away and give them a time limit, no more than 180 days, to produce a framework for a new juvenile justice system. I offer one of my senior prosecutors to this effort.

The reformers should be nonpartisan; this is not about politics. It is about making California a safe, desirable place to live.

II

Society has a primary duty to punish juvenile offenders, not to rehabilitate them.

The punishment of boot camp, life imprisonment or execution should fit the viciousness of the crime, not the age of the violent offender. As a society, we cannot show any sympathy for, or accept any excuses from, the young thugs, perverts and psychopaths who are destroying our schools and neighborhoods.

Thousands of young violent offenders have no moral compass and no fear of punishment. Worst of all, many have no sense of right and wrong. The statistics are shocking and grim. According to *Uniform Crime Reports for the United States,* in 1992, 2,829 juveniles were arrested for murder, 5,369 for forcible rape, 40,434 for robbery and 63,777 for aggravated assault. The National Crime Victimization Survey conducted a few years ago by the federal Justice Department estimated that some 430,000 children had been the victims of rape, robbery or assault at school. *These* are the children we must protect—not those who lack religious beliefs, eat the wrong diet, were abused by a family member or were driven to violence by television or music. Those are not valid reasons for our citizens to live in perpetual fear of evil kids and violent juvenile offenders.

Do the Crime, Serve the Time

What can we do? Curfews for young people in shopping malls and other public areas should be instituted. And all of the estimated 270,000 children who bring a gun or a knife to school each day should be sent to boot camp for six months. Any juvenile who uses a deadly weapon in committing a crime should be given a mandatory one-year prison sentence.

Juveniles arrested for crimes like 1993's rape and murder of two girls in Houston, or the heartless murder of three innocent boys in Arkansas, should not be let off by too-lenient courts or age-mandated early-release programs. They should serve time like adults and even face the prospect of society's ultimate solution for violent offenders—no matter what their age. Juveniles 14 or older must be tried as adults for violent crimes involving rape, murder, armed robbery, and aggravated assault.

The first lesson that should be taught in school is: You do the crime, you serve the time. Parents, teachers and society as a whole will not enjoy peace of mind until our schools and streets are free of violent juveniles.

"Imprisonment in the adult system . . . for acts committed while in adolescence may be irrational and may even contribute to . . . criminality."

Fewer Juveniles Should Be Tried as Adults

Coalition for Juvenile Justice

The Coalition for Juvenile Justice is a governmental committee that was created in 1974 to advise the president and Congress on issues related to juvenile justice and the prevention of juvenile crime. In the following viewpoint, the coalition objects to the increasingly common practice of trying and punishing juveniles as adults. According to the coalition, juveniles held in adult institutions are more likely to be abused and less likely to receive rehabilitative services than those held in juvenile institutions. While the coalition concedes that some youths should be tried and sentenced as adults, it argues that this approach should be reserved as a last resort and must be instituted fairly and humanely.

As you read, consider the following questions:

1. Why were separate court and treatment systems created for juveniles and adults, as explained by the coalition?
2. According to Martin Forst and his colleagues, as quoted by the coalition, what are the social costs of transferring juveniles to the adult justice system?
3. What type of approach does the coalition propose as an alternative to trying juveniles as adults?

There are no easy answers to the serious problems presented by the increasing violence against, and by, our children and youth. Simplistic pleas for a return to those family values that were portrayed on television in the 1960s, for the total transformation and reformation of our cities, for a transfer of all serious offenders from the juvenile court to an adult criminal justice system that is less effective in reducing crime and less humane than the juvenile system, or for a banning of all guns without reducing our nation's commitment to violence as a lifestyle will not succeed in addressing a highly complex problem.

With these words, our 1992 report on serious, violent, and chronic juvenile offenders urged policymakers at both the federal and state levels to take a rational and measured approach to the increasing problem of juvenile delinquency. Unfortunately, our words seem to have fallen on deaf ears as the trend toward reliance on transfer to adult criminal court and prosecution as adults as the main responses to serious and violent juvenile crime has accelerated. . . .

Much of the recent legislative response to juvenile crime is a political reaction to public opinion fueled by disproportionate media coverage of youth crime. It also reflects the belief that the juvenile justice system is ineffective. Research belies this belief. Studies show that only about eighteen percent of those juveniles with police contact persist in delinquent behavior, and fifty-nine percent of those juveniles referred to juvenile or family court have only that one referral. Even high-risk juvenile offenders do not remain high-risk for long; serious juvenile crime peaks between sixteen and seventeen years of age, and the prevalence of serious violence drops dramatically after age twenty. Thus, imprisonment in the adult system for incapacitation purposes for long periods of time for acts committed while in adolescence may be irrational and may even contribute to a longer period of criminality.

The Coalition for Juvenile Justice urges that policy makers at all levels of government address the complex problem of juvenile crime, even serious and violent juvenile crime, in a more careful and reasoned fashion without succumbing to the "easy answers" advocated by those who may have particular political agendas. We also urge that coherent efforts to enhance the prevention of delinquent behavior be treated seriously by legislators, rather than simply being lumped together as "pork barrel" schemes on the legislative floor or in the media. . . .

Juveniles Are Different

As a preliminary matter, it must be recalled that the juvenile or family court is uniquely an American invention in its inception. The juvenile justice system was established in recognition of the fact that children and adolescents are quite different from adults, not just in size or physical maturity but also developmentally. Young people were deemed to be capable of being rehabilitated and changed, and they also were also thought to be particularly vulnerable to physical or sexual abuse and to negative influences by adults in the criminal justice system. That is largely why separate court and treatment systems were created, and that is why separation from adults and jail removal have been central policies in the Juvenile Justice and Delinquency Prevention Act of 1974 from an early point in its history.

Sentences for Juveniles Tried as Adults in Virginia (1988–1990)

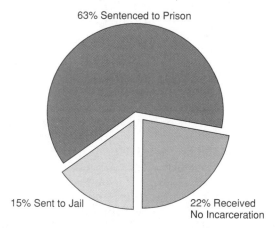

63% Sentenced to Prison

15% Sent to Jail

22% Received No Incarceration

Source: Virginia Commission on Youth, *The Study of Serious Juvenile Offenders*, 1993.

Although states have long permitted transfer or waiver to the adult court as a sort of "safety valve" for the juvenile justice system, this alternative was to serve as a last resort for recalcitrant juveniles, almost as a recognition of failure. Thus, transfer was to be resorted to in only the most extreme cases and with full recognition that the adult criminal justice system was even more overcrowded and was less effective in changing the behavior of its offenders than the juvenile justice system. With those basic premises stated, we can address the current issues around the placement of juveniles in the adult courts. . . .

Detention and Delay

Once a juvenile is transferred from the juvenile or family court, the youth will almost always be kept locked up, either in

182

a juvenile detention home or in an adult jail or other adult facility. Frequently, the youth will be moved to an adult facility and will remain there until the disposition of the charge in the adult court. Although the juvenile may be kept separate and apart from adults, this is not always the case, even though the charges may be dismissed or the youth may be acquitted. Indeed, the data show that the conviction rate in adult courts is generally lower than that in juvenile or family courts, and the charges are often "plea bargained" down in seriousness. There is also considerably more delay in the criminal court process than in the juvenile justice system, and so the periods of incarceration in a secure facility, whether adult or juvenile, will be significantly longer than for youths in safer juvenile programs.

Related to the issue of detention and length of pretrial incarceration is the longer time consumed by processing in the criminal system. The major comparative study by Dr. Jeffrey Fagan demonstrated that "punishment" is less swift through adult processing than in juvenile processing. Juveniles in New York who begin in adult court take 145 days from arrest to sentencing as contrasted with 100 days until disposition for youths charged with comparable offenses in juvenile courts in New Jersey. A study by Cary Rudman and others also showed that it took an average of 246 days for violent youths to be transferred to, convicted in, and sentenced by the criminal court as opposed to an average 98 days for juvenile court processing, thus undermining the frequent pleas for swift and sure justice. Practically all these youths are in secure detention or jail during the pendency of the proceedings. The average length of stay for juveniles in detention in Wayne County, Michigan, awaiting trial in adult court after waiver is 200 days. Thus, although developmental psychologists tell us that the swiftness of the sanction is crucial to meaningful behavior modification among children and adolescents, criminal court processing ignores that acknowledged fact. Juvenile courts are much more likely to impose immediate sanctions than the adult criminal courts and thus can impact more profoundly on the juvenile offenders.

Sentencing

The changes in transfer and waiver statutes have had a major impact on the overcrowded adult court as well. In Florida, for example, the number of youths in adult court rose from 904 in 1975–76 to 2,883 in 1981 82 to 5,877 in 1989–90. Although some early studies showed that those juveniles transferred to the adult criminal justice system received relatively short sentences to incarceration, or no incarceration at all, more recent studies show that juveniles are now receiving more severe sanctions in the adult court than youths with similar charges receive

183

in the juvenile court. [*The Study of Serious Juvenile Offenders* by the Virginia Commission on Youth] showed that of the more than 1,000 juveniles transferred to adult court from 1988 to 1990, sixty-three percent were sentenced to prison, fifteen percent were sent to a local jail, and twenty-two percent received no incarceration. The average sentence was 8.1 years, but of the juveniles released from adult or juvenile institutions during this time period, those tried as adults actually served an average of seventeen months as contrasted with 7.6 months of time served for those in juvenile learning centers. Other studies show a wide disparity in results in criminal courts, with some studies showing a low rate of conviction for the charged violent offense and others showing a high conviction rate and for the offense originally charged rather than a lesser offense. A Utah study showed that of the fifty-three juveniles sent to adult court over a five-year period ending in June, 1993, forty-nine cases went forward and forty of those forty-nine were plea bargained, with only nine being subjected to a trial. Sixteen of the youths never went to prison, and twenty-eight others received prison sentences that resulted in their serving only about two years of incarceration. Only five of the fifty-three will spend any extended period of time in prison beyond their twenty-first birthdays, and mostly for homicide.

Significant findings are based on comparisons of youth and adult treatment of juveniles in the area of corrections and on comparisons of recidivism rates in the two systems. Juveniles in adult institutions are five times more likely to be sexually assaulted, twice as likely to be beaten by staff, and fifty percent more likely to be attacked with a weapon than youths in a juvenile facility. The same studies also indicate a much lower rating of counseling programs, of efforts to improve family relations, and of medical care in adult corrections than in juvenile institutions. The youth facilities also were rated much higher in promoting social and personal development through inmate and staff interaction. This obviously reflects the dichotomy between treatment and custody in the two programs, but it also has major implications for future behaviors. Martin Forst, Jeffrey Fagan and T. Scott Vivona noted that "although transfer decreases community risks through lengthy incapacitation of violent youngsters, it carries both fiscal and social costs. The social costs of imprisoning young offenders in adult facilities may be paid in later crime and violence upon their release."

Two different studies over a ten-year period show significantly higher recidivism rates for youths tried in adult courts versus those tried in juvenile courts for the same offenses and with similar personal profiles. Fagan's 1991 study, for example, demonstrated that teenagers tried as adults in New York had a

184

higher recidivism rate than comparable youths tried as juveniles in New Jersey for the same offenses, and they re-offended sooner, committed more serious new offenses, and were re-incarcerated more frequently.

The more punitive treatment of serious juvenile offenders through transfer or placement in adult criminal courts arguably would seem to have some deterrent effect on youths contemplating such activities. However, it may be instructive that the two jurisdictions with the most punitive systems for dealing with juveniles, New York and Florida, are still the two states with the highest crime rates. The draconian laws in Illinois have had no impact on serious juvenile delinquency in Cook County. As Simon Singer and David McDowall have pointed out, adolescents are less influenced by general deterrence, and juveniles in New York were "not responsive" to the more punitive nature of that state's Juvenile Offender Law, in spite of widespread publicity. Eric Jensen and Linda Metsger reached similar conclusions in studying the deterrent effects of a 1981 automatic waiver statute enacted in Idaho, a vastly different jurisdiction. Comparing Idaho with two neighboring states with transfer statutes similar to that in effect in Idaho prior to 1981, juvenile violent crime rates went down in Wyoming and Montana while they went up in Idaho, thus suggesting the failure of deterrence as a result of the new statute.

Capital Punishment

America is one of only three nations in the world that currently allow the execution of persons for crimes committed while they were children. The others are Iran and Iraq. As of May 1, 1994, there were thirty-four persons on death row under capital sentences for crimes committed as juveniles in this country. Since 1979, only fourteen juvenile executions have occurred worldwide—nine in the United States and the other five in Bangladesh, Rwanda, Pakistan, and Barbados, nations that have since abandoned the practice by signing or ratifying the United Nations Convention on the Rights of the Child. In addition to departing from the standards of the rest of the world in determining the appropriateness of the ultimate penalty for children, the imposition of the death penalty ignores the substantial evidence of the greater vulnerability and impulsivity of youth and of the false sense of omnipotence and immortality that many juveniles have. The study by Dr. Dorothy Lewis and others of fourteen juveniles on death rows in the United States shows that these children universally have "a battery of psychological, emotional, and other problems going to their likely capacity for judgment and level of blameworthiness." Almost all the children had a history of serious physical or sexual abuse, and many have suffered severe head injuries during childhood. For many of these reasons, the United Nations Convention on the Rights of the Child has disapproved of the execution of those who committed crimes while under the age of eighteen. The National Coalition for Juvenile Justice unanimously endorsed American ratification of the Convention at our 1992 Annual Spring Conference, thus reaffirming our earlier resolution, also unanimously adopted in September, 1989, calling for abolition of the death penalty for juveniles. . . .

The Coalition regularly reaffirms its commitment to delinquency prevention as a crucial element in addressing the problem of growing delinquency rates and, ultimately, serious and violent crime. . . . Prevention is still the most cost-effective and humane method of addressing the problem of delinquent behavior. We must identify continually those prevention programs which work and commit resources to replicate those programs in other states and localities. The Coalition believes that delinquency prevention should continue to be at the top of the agenda. . . .

There also must be an increased emphasis on the development of more community-centered and family-based programs, especially in those urban core communities where "at risk" most often means "high risk." It is desirable to focus more on intervention for those populations that are most vulnerable for delinquency or for children who first show signs of problems, but we must be careful to avoid the labelling that sometimes becomes a self-fulfilling prophecy. . . .

We do need to focus more as a society on the recapture of a sense of personal responsibility and adherence to simple virtue. The noted social commentators James Q. Wilson and Richard Herrnstein have said "how we spend money on schools, job training, or welfare programs may be less important than the message accompanying such expenditures: Do we appear to be rewarding the acceptance or the rejection of personal responsibility?" However, we also need to reaffirm the importance of the community and acknowledge, in the words of the African proverb, that "it takes a whole village to raise a child.". . .

We must be prepared to act and not simply react. We must get smart about juvenile crime, and not just get tough. And we should not abandon a juvenile justice system that has numerous models of programs that work in order to access an adult criminal justice system that is financially and programmatically bankrupt. . . . Where trial as an adult is necessary as a last resort for those hard-core youth who commit the most serious crimes, the method of selection must be objective and rational, and they should be placed in correctional institutions that are humane, safe, and enriched with programs to give youthful inmates a chance to be good citizens in the future.

> "*Curfews are necessary to keep our children safe from crime. And, as courts have agreed, they can be constitutional if properly drafted.*"

Curfews Can Be Effective and Constitutional

William Ruefle, Kenneth Mike Reynolds, and Overtis Hicks Brantley

Curfew laws have been criticized for violating the constitutional rights of minors. In Part I of the following two-part viewpoint, William Ruefle and Kenneth Mike Reynolds point out that while some curfew laws have been deemed unconstitutional due to vagueness and overreach, they have not been found to violate young people's constitutional rights. In Part II of the viewpoint, Overtis Hicks Brantley argues that the restrictions imposed by curfew legislation are minor and are justified by the need to prevent juvenile crime. Ruefle is an assistant professor in the Department of Political Science and Criminal Justice at the University of South Alabama. Reynolds is a research associate at the College of Urban and Public Affairs at the University of New Orleans. Brantley has served as the acting deputy city attorney for the city of Atlanta, Georgia.

As you read, consider the following questions:

1. What three assumptions are curfew laws based on, according to Ruefle and Reynolds?
2. According to Brantley, why did the 5th U.S. Circuit Court of Appeals uphold Dallas's curfew?

From William Ruefle and Kenneth Mike Reynolds, "Curfews and Delinquency in Major American Cities," *Crime & Delinquency*, July 1995. Copyright ©1995 by Sage Publications. Reprinted by permission Sage Publications. Overtis Hicks Brantley, "Curfews for Juveniles: Yes, Safety Is a Fundamental Right," *ABA Journal*, April 1994. Copyright 1994 by the American Bar Association. Reprinted with permission.

I

In 1972, the Board of Trustees of the National Council on Crime and Delinquency (NCCD) published a policy statement on juvenile curfews that opposed the adoption of new curfews and urged the repeal of existing ones. It argued that curfew enforcement is ineffective and discriminatory toward both minority and lower socioeconomic status youths, that curfew laws are legally doubtful on constitutional grounds, and that their main impact is to unnecessarily involve large numbers of nondelinquent youths with the criminal justice system, that is, net widening. The fact that the 1967 *Task Force Report: Juvenile Delinquency and Youth Crime* of the President's Crime Commission made no mention of curfews as an effective method for either preventing or controlling delinquency was cited as further evidence against curfews.

The NCCD trustees urged the adoption of two policies aimed at decreasing the potential for involvement with the juvenile justice system. The first was the establishment of Youth Service Bureaus, designed to divert youth away from the justice system and toward existing social service resources in a community. The other was the removal of status offenders from the jurisdiction of the juvenile court. Both of these priorities were part of a larger noninterventionist reform movement that stressed diversion, deinstitutionalization, decriminalization, and due process. This hands-off approach to reform was bolstered at the national level through the passage of the Juvenile Justice and Delinquency Prevention Act of 1974, and through the work of the National Advisory Committee on Criminal Justice Standards and Goals, whose 1976 *Report of the Task Force on Juvenile Justice and Delinquency Prevention* made no mention of curfews as a means to prevent delinquency.

However, since the mid-1970s there has also been a competing policy agenda for juvenile justice reform, the "just deserts" model that stresses accountability, more severe sentencing, determinate sentencing, continued reliance on state training schools to control chronic offenders, and greater reliance on transfer to adult court. Municipal curfew ordinances fall within this crime control approach to juvenile justice. . . .

The Logic of Curfews

A curfew is a social control mechanism. The common assumptions underlying it and other such mechanisms are: (a) human beings must be controlled if society is to be orderly and safe, (b) society has a consensus on a set of appropriate values and behaviors, and (c) absent internally motivated voluntary compliance, people can be forced to comply through external control mechanisms. City officials who support curfews believe they

188

have a compelling interest to reduce juvenile crime and victimization, while promoting juvenile safety and well-being.

Proponents of curfews argue that they serve as a tool for both the police and parents. In high-crime communities, curfews are a means to protect nondelinquent youth from crime and to deny delinquent youth the opportunity to engage in crime. In low-crime communities, they provide the police with the means to disperse late-night crowds of juveniles, to stop and question youths during curfew hours, and, if necessary, to keep youths off the streets. For parents, curfews provide support and legitimization for restrictions on the late-night activities of their children. Without curfews, it is much more difficult for parents to place such restrictions on their children when other youngsters in the neighborhood are out late at night.

No Violation of Rights

Municipal curfew ordinances often have been challenged on constitutional grounds, usually by the local chapter of the American Civil Liberties Union. The primary objections are that curfews violate the Equal Protection Clause by setting up a suspect classification based on age, and that they result in selective enforcement to the detriment of minority youths. Curfews also have been challenged on the grounds that they infringe on the fundamental rights of free movement and free association, and of family privacy in child-rearing. Another argument is that curfews violate due-process rights through seizure of persons by police without probable cause and through forced confessions in answering police questions. However, when curfew laws have been declared unconstitutional, it has been because of their vagueness and overreach, not because of any violation of equal-protection guarantees, fundamental rights, or procedural due process. For example, in *Johnson v. Opelousas, La.*, a municipal curfew ordinance was held unconstitutional because it was overly restrictive, too broadly applied, and did not allow for any exceptions—not because of any violation of fundamental rights.

In the case *Qutb v. Strauss*, the United States Fifth Circuit Court of Appeals applied strict scrutiny review to a 1991 Dallas curfew and overturned a lower court order enjoining the enforcement of the ordinance. The Dallas ordinance applied to youths 16 years of age and younger, with certain exceptions, from 11 p.m. to 6 a.m. weeknights, and from midnight to 6 a.m. on weekend nights. The majority held there was no violation of the Equal Protection Clause because Dallas clearly established a nexus between its compelling interests in delinquency prevention and reduction of juvenile victimization, and the age classification created by the ordinance. The nexus was established with data presented by the city that demonstrated that the delinquency rate for an age cohort increases proportionately from the 10th to the 16th year of age, and that in the year preceding the curfew Dallas had experienced an increase in both property offenses and serious violent offenses by juveniles. Evidence also was presented that showed that past murders, aggravated assaults, and rapes most often occurred during the hours covered by the curfew, and that 31% of the robberies took place on streets and highways. This evidence convinced the court that the classification created by the ordinance was narrowly tailored to fit a compelling interest of the state.

Spreading Like Blockbusters

The youth of Laurel, Maryland, aren't into assault weapons; there's no local chapter of the Crips and Bloods. But when graffiti appeared on the side of the 7-Eleven and residents griped about their vandalized cars, the city council did what it could: it imposed a curfew on kids 15 and under after 11 p.m. on weekdays. . . .

Curfews are spreading through suburban America faster than Blockbuster Videos. In locales like Laurel, where the streets aren't exactly mean, they mainly provide psychological comfort for worried parents and neighbors. But urban areas reeling from serious juvenile crime are rediscovering them, too. One fourth of the nation's 200 largest cities imposed curfews in the 1990s; others are suddenly enforcing laws that have been on the books for years.

Melinda Beck, *Newsweek*, July 17, 1995.

Crucial to the constitutional success of the Dallas curfew was the fact that it contained numerous defenses that allowed minors to remain in public places during curfew hours. Exceptions to the curfew were allowed if a youth was accompanied by a parent or an adult authorized by a parent; engaged in interstate travel; returning home from a school, religious, or civic-sponsored function; was on the sidewalk in front of his or her home or the home of a neighbor; or exercising First Amendment rights. These exceptions convinced the court that the ordinance was the least restrictive means of accomplishing the city's goals, and thus represented only minimal intrusion on the parental right to rear their children without undue government influence.

The court also spoke to another potential constitutional issue: limited geographical construction. The majority opinion reflected that a narrowly drawn nocturnal juvenile ordinance that applies only in a municipality's high-risk, high-crime areas or danger zones would not be unconstitutional. This 1993 ruling on the Dallas curfew, and the subsequent refusal by the United

States Supreme Court to review it, provided a legal foundation for existing ordinances and stimulated numerous other cities to enact curfews for the first time.

II

In the city of Atlanta, the need for a curfew became apparent after two children were killed just days apart. The first, a 4-year-old, lay asleep in bed when she became the innocent victim of teens involved in a drive-by shooting. The second child, age 13, was gunned down in a case of mistaken identity while standing on a street corner at 4:15 a.m.

Following these incidents, outraged parents demanded better protection for their children, and the city responded by enacting a curfew ordinance in November 1990.

My job was assisting Atlanta Councilwoman Davetta Johnson in writing a law that would withstand constitutional challenge. At the time, my interest in the issue was purely legal. But all that's changed since I've become a parent. Like many other parents, I now realize that curfews are necessary to keep our children safe from crime. And, as courts have agreed, they can be constitutional if properly drafted.

Passing Scrutiny from the Courts

Under the law, the constitutional rights of adults and minors are not protected equally. Minor rights can be regulated to a greater degree. Because curfews implicate fundamental rights, however, courts generally have subjected curfews to strict scrutiny. Under strict scrutiny, a curfew can only be upheld if it is narrowly tailored to serve a compelling governmental interest.

There's no doubt that reducing juvenile crime and promoting juvenile safety qualify as compelling interests. The next question is whether the curfew is narrowly drawn. Courts have interpreted that to mean the curfew cannot infringe on certain fundamental rights.

For instance, the 5th U.S. Circuit Court of Appeals recently upheld a curfew adopted by the city of Dallas, which prohibits juveniles from remaining in public places between the hours of 11 p.m. and 6 a.m. on weeknights, and from 12 midnight until 6 a.m. on weekends.

The curfew was found to be reasonable because it used the least restrictive means of accomplishing its goals by exempting juveniles who were: 1) accompanied by a parent or guardian; 2) engaging in core First Amendment activity; 3) traveling to or from employment; 4) engaged in interstate commerce; or 5) responding to an emergency.

The only activity that the Dallas law limits is aimless, senseless hanging out on street corners in the middle of the night. As this law demonstrates, curfews do not violate the due process rights of juveniles when appropriate exemptions are incorporated.

Some have argued that curfews can be abused and used as a means to harass and intimidate, but the Atlanta experience is just the opposite. Through proper training, the Atlanta police force has been taught to view the curfew as a method to protect children, not to bully them. Children are taken home to their parents whenever possible, rather than to juvenile detention. Instead of filling out an arrest warrant, the officers conduct field interviews.

Atlanta Police Chief Eldrin Bell touched the heart of the matter when he told his troops: "Our goal is to engender positive contacts between police, parents and children. Our intent is to improve the safety of our children and to support and underscore parental authority."

No right is absolute. I view a properly drafted, properly enforced curfew as a minor restraint on our right to life, liberty and the pursuit of happiness. If only one child is saved by a curfew, isn't it worth it?

"Even if minority neighborhoods are made safer by curfew measures, the use of curfews may reinforce deeply held stereotypes of minorities as criminals."

Curfews May Be Ineffective and Discriminatory

Harvard Law Review

Many communities have begun to enforce curfews in an attempt to control juvenile crime. In the following viewpoint, the editors of the *Harvard Law Review* examine curfews through the lens of "critical race theory," which holds that racism pervades America's institutions, including the criminal justice system. When considered from the perspective of critical race theory, according to the editors, the decision to impose curfews can be seen as stemming from society's racist tendency to perceive minority youths as criminals. Furthermore, the editors contend, because the imposition of curfews disproportionately affects minorities, such policies can be viewed as a form of discriminatory harassment.

As you read, consider the following questions:

1. According to the viewpoint, what has curfew enforcement cost the community of Hartford?
2. What arguments do critics make in support of their opposition to curfews, as listed in the viewpoint?
3. In the authors' opinion, what is wrong with using curfews as a "war model" against gangs?

In response to the problem of gang violence, governments and communities have launched an onslaught of measures that have varied in their effectiveness. Police have employed stop and search policies, road blocks, and special gang profiles designed to target suspected gang members. Prosecutors have creatively used existing and new legislation to find grounds for trial, including application of the Racketeer Influenced Corrupt Organizations Act (RICO) to gangs, parental liability for the actions of children, enforcement of new anti-gang statutes like California's Street Terrorism Enforcement and Protection Act, and prosecution of gangs as public nuisances. New legislation provides for stiffer sentences, and judges enjoin gang activities. Policymakers also seek longer-term social solutions through special education and job programs, counseling, alternative recreational activities, and official attempts to cooperate and negotiate with gangs. Efforts to improve employment, housing, and health conditions complement gang-specific measures.

Juvenile curfews fall into an intermediate category of measures that regulate "legitimate" conduct that is seen as related to criminal gang activity. In addition to curfews, public schools have banned gang clothing, and towns have passed tailored anti-loitering ordinances. Curfews and these other measures lie between traditional law enforcement and longer-term efforts to address the underlying social decay that spurs gang formation.

Juvenile curfews have been one remarkably prevalent policy chosen by cities across the country. New curfews have been enacted and existing curfews revived in Detroit, Los Angeles, Milwaukee, Philadelphia, Newark, Atlanta, Buffalo, Miami, Phoenix, and Little Rock. San Francisco, New Orleans, and Birmingham have witnessed a rise in pro-curfew sentiment. Washington, D.C., enacted a curfew that was struck down in the courts, but a new curfew in Dallas survived a legal challenge. Each city's curfew varies in its particulars. Each covers different age groups, restricts different hours, applies different sanctions, and permits different exceptions to the curfew. Understanding how juvenile curfews work in at least one city is essential to a textured assessment of their benefits and drawbacks.

One Example: Hartford, Connecticut

In Hartford, Connecticut, the two largest youth gangs have been at war for years. Violence peaked in the summer of 1993, when the Latin Kings and Los Solidos gangs escalated their attacks and murdered rival gang members and shot innocent bystanders. In the hardest hit neighborhoods, many residents were afraid to leave their homes or to let their children out of the house unattended. On September 8, 1993, the Hartford city council instructed police to begin enforcing a citywide curfew that banned youths under fifteen years of age from city streets after nine o'clock at night. Eight days later, the city council unanimously voted to raise the curfew age to include all youths under the age of eighteen. Minors caught violating the ordinance are to be returned to their parents, who are then subject to a ninety-dollar fine or jail. The measure generally seems to have reduced the violence and brought some quiet to Hartford's neighborhoods. As one resident explained, "It's almost like a police state, which I like."

The relative peace, however, has cost community life and individual freedom. A police officer called one Hartford neighborhood "a ghost town." A reporter described the city streets as "virtually deserted." Residents—particularly young Hispanic males who match police profiles of gang members—suffer frequent police stops and questioning. The Connecticut Civil Liberties Union (CCLU) has expressed concern that the curfew and police actions may violate the federal Constitution. Nevertheless, even some CCLU board members believe that the emergency situation justifies the curfew. Most residents seem willing to trade some personal freedom for a measure of security and relative peace. As a neighborhood organizer explained, "A lot of these folks . . . talking about civil liberties, et cetera, don't live here, and if they want to have no curfew in their neighborhoods, that's fine. . . . [I]n this community, the people who live here should have a right to determine how they want to live."

The Policy Debate

The immediate purpose of curfews in Hartford and other cities is to keep juveniles off the streets, both for their own safety and to prevent the loitering associated with gangs and gang delinquency. Curfews give police an added weapon to detain suspicious youth and preempt potentially criminal activity. Although children who are not in gangs might have to alter their behavior to comply with the curfew, proponents of the curfew argue that the concession is not too great given that most curfew ordinances do not apply if the juvenile is traveling with a parent, commuting to or from work, or attending organized activities. Curfew supporters emphasize the potential increase in public safety that can result. Besides making the streets safe for the public, community confidence and morale can be boosted by demonstrating that something is being done about the community's problems. A ceasefire in gang fighting might even allow community redevelopment efforts to begin.

Critics of the curfew counter that juvenile curfews require innocent children and their families to rearrange their daily lives and to sacrifice a measure of personal freedom even if the curfews allow for reasonable exceptions. The more a curfew's hours are extended, its age groups broadened, and its exceptions limited, the more it disrupts legitimate activities. Curfew enforcement also diverts scarce police and administrative resources from more serious criminal activity. Despite the expenditures, those intent on breaking the law may not even be deterred by a curfew, either because of the curfew ordinance's limited sanctions or a general indifference on the part of targeted youths to threats of criminal punishment. Also, increased police stops and questioning performed during investigations of possible curfew violations might further strain tenuous citizen/police relations More seriously, selective enforcement of a curfew could present a very real danger of discrimination, particularly against the many innocent young minority males who match overly inclusive gang-member profiles that are based primarily on race. Rather than improve community welfare, then, curfews might exacerbate community tensions and worsen morale.

Supporters and detractors differ further over whether curfews aggravate or ameliorate the underlying social conditions that foster gang involvement. Curfews might support parents' efforts to control and to nurture their children, or alternatively, might force less-involved parents to take more responsibility for the welfare and behavior of their children. In other ways, however, curfews might undermine parental authority by interjecting the state into family affairs and by reducing parental accountability and flexibility. Curfews also might diminish the self-esteem and personal development of young people by preventing them from making their own decisions. Empirical evidence remains inconclusive, and scholars are thus unable to resolve the controversy surrounding the actual effects of curfews. . . .

Critical Race Theory

Critical race theory underscores the fundamental role of race in social relations and how the dynamic of racial inequality informs and is affected by social and legal policy. Racism is a central fact of American existence and shapes how individuals and groups experience the law and in particular the criminal law. The law remains constructed by dominant groups, and racial stereotypes and discriminatory motives often infect the formulation and enforcement of the law.

The protection of civil liberties or formal rights may not be able to remedy racial inequality; if everyone is given equal rights in an unequal system, the resulting outcome will be predetermined. Yet rights can advance minority interests when situated in a considered consciousness about race. Once reconceived, rights are compatible with efforts to advance racial communities and racial identity. Community-centered theories must be similarly reconceived. They have tended to pay inadequate

196

attention to the problems of entrenched racial inequality; the ideal of community deliberation has failed to give weight to the exclusion of blacks and other minorities from the conception of community. Theories that accommodate an understanding of the needs of minority communities can advance those communities' interests.

People Power Needed

Curfews alone cannot address the complex problems posed by hard-core gangstas and street crews. Only consistent and substantive adult intervention and supervision will work. . . .

We need people power—folks working individually with children and youth—if we are ever to change the violent teenage behavior that we are finally coming to understand is not exclusive to urban youth.

Adrienne T. Washington, *Washington Times*, September 26, 1995.

Viewed through the lens of critical race theory, the initial choice to impose curfews and to devote special energy to cracking down on gangs appears motivated by racial bias or stereotypes. Critical race scholars are skeptical of efforts to justify repressive law enforcement measures by pointing to high crime rates. Some scholars have noted that, notwithstanding the existence of gang violence, society has overreacted in what can be called a "moral panic." The reaction may be driven by images of minorities as criminals and a lack of empathy for the problems and pressures facing inner-city youth. Curfews fit into a pattern of law enforcement that focuses on suppressing gang violence but that neglects the social causes of gangs. Curfews may exhibit the majority's belief that poor and predominantly minority communities need to be regulated or controlled by others. The danger that the choice to employ curfews is infected with racial bias or stereotyping remains even if the curfew is chosen or supported by the minority community itself, if the community consciously or unconsciously endorses majority beliefs.

Once curfews are imposed, the burden falls disproportionately on minority individuals and communities. Police resources are concentrated and curfews most stringently enforced in neighborhoods with large minority populations because that is where gang activity is often highest. Minority youths, who often match race-based police profiles of gang members, are detained and singled out for harassment. Even if minority neighborhoods are made safer by curfew measures, the use of curfews may reinforce deeply held stereotypes of minorities as criminals or as morally inferior and in need of special supervision.

Critical race theory offers more than just a heightened sense of the downside of juvenile curfews, however. A sharpened sensitivity to the relationship between the gang problem, community responses, and the dynamic of racial and social inequality emphasizes that curfews should not be just another effort to criminalize the symptoms of deeper social problems. Evidence suggests that using curfews as part of a law enforcement "war model" against gangs oversimplifies the issues and is not effective in reducing crime. A more complete solution should recognize that there are understandable reasons for delinquent behavior in an oppressed minority population. . . .

Possibilities and Perils

Curfews remain a limited and inadequate response to the problems of gangs. Critical race theory indicates a deeper need to spur community revival than curfews can offer. Critical race theory in particular demands policies and programs that address the gang problem but that avoid merely criminalizing behavior that is rooted in social phenomena partially outside the control of minority individuals. Specific programs could build on the potential for curfews to encourage family cohesion, but the programs should be directed by the communities themselves, even if they are supported from without, to avoid fostering stereotypes of minority communities as criminal and incapable of self-regulation. . . .

It is too simplistic to say that curfews are good or bad; curfews present both possibilities and perils and should be considered as one option in an array of short- and long-term strategies. Constructive programs that rebuild support structures for young people growing up in urban centers, more than the quick fix of curfews, can enable both individual and community self-determination and avoid an inevitably unsatisfactory balancing of individual and community interests. Curfews, if chosen, should be part of a comprehensive response to the social and economic ills that beset urban areas and must not become an end in themselves.

Periodical Bibliography

The following articles have been selected to supplement the diverse views presented in this chapter. Addresses are provided for periodicals not indexed in the *Readers' Guide to Periodical Literature*, the *Alternative Press Index*, or the *Social Sciences Index*.

Peter Annin	"'Superpredators' Arrive: Should We Cage the New Breed of Vicious Kids?" *Newsweek*, January 22, 1996.
Melissa Caudle	"Eight Ways to Safer Schools," *Education Digest*, December 1994.
Celeste Fremon	"Tough Love: In East L.A.'s Most Violent Neighborhood Mothers Unite to Save Their Children," *Utne Reader*, March/April 1996.
Sarah van Gelder	"Reclaiming Kids," *In Context*, no. 38, Spring 1994.
Sarah Glazer	"Juvenile Justice," *CQ Researcher*, February 25, 1994. Available from 1414 22nd St. NW, Washington, DC 20037.
Jet	"Should Good Parents Be Jailed When Bad Children Break Laws?" June 27, 1994.
Lane Nelson	"Death Watch: Killing Kids," *Angolite*, November/December 1995. Available from Louisiana State Penitentiary, Angola, LA 70712.
New York Times	"What Can Be Done About the Scourge of Violence Among Juveniles?" December 30, 1994.
Jill Smolowe	"Going Soft on Crime," *Time*, November 14, 1994.
Christopher Swope	"Tracking Down Truants," *Governing*, August 1995.
Joseph B. Treaster	"Beyond Probation: Breaking the Cycle of Juvenile Arrests," *New York Times*, December 29, 1994.
USA Today	"Reducing Number of Repeat Offenders," April 1994.
Laurel Shaper Walters	"States Try to Rewrite Crime and Punishment," *Christian Science Monitor*, December 5, 1995. Available from Reprints, 1 Norway St., Boston, MA 02115.

For Further Discussion

Chapter 1

1. Margaret O. Hyde uses statistics to support her contention that juvenile crime and violence are increasing. Michael A. Jones and Barry Krisberg also rely on statistics in arguing that juvenile crime and violence are not increasing. Whose use of statistics is more effective? Cite examples from the viewpoints to support your answer.

2. Hyde cites anecdotal evidence as well as statistics in her viewpoint. Is this anecdotal information more or less persuasive than the statistics? Explain.

3. Merrica Turner provides a firsthand account of her experience as a high school student to argue that juvenile violence is a serious problem in public schools. How does her description compare with your own school environment? Do you find Turner's narrative believable? Why or why not?

4. Michele Ingrassia's viewpoint originally appeared as a *Newsweek* article in which Ingrassia described several incidents in order to illustrate her view that adolescents are increasingly brutal and remorseless. Susan Douglas argues that reports such as Ingrassia's are part of a campaign by politicians and the media to blame teenagers for society's problems. Which viewpoint is more convincing, and why?

Chapter 2

1. Mortimer B. Zuckerman argues that viewing television violence has a negative impact on children. How does Laurence Jarvik respond to this argument? Whose viewpoint is more tenable, and why?

2. In this chapter, the authors discuss a variety of potential causes of juvenile crime and violence. Of the factors discussed, do you think some are more important than others? Support your answer with references to the viewpoints.

3. Of the authors who discuss the causes of inner-city juvenile crime and violence in this chapter, which ones focus on the economic and social conditions of these areas, and which emphasize the moral values of inner-city residents? Do any authors address both issues? Whose analysis of inner-city juvenile crime is the most convincing? Explain your answer.

Chapter 3

1. The authors in this chapter present various possible reasons for why young people become involved in gang-related crime. List the reasons in order of importance, and explain your assessment of the importance of each reason. Can you think of any reasons that are not given in the chapter? What are they?

2. Roger H. Davis is a retired FBI agent. Does knowing this aspect of his background influence your evaluation of his viewpoint? If so, how?

3. After reading the viewpoints in this chapter, do you think that most teenagers who become involved in gangs do so by choice or because of circumstances beyond their control? Support your answer with examples from the viewpoints.

Chapter 4

1. John J. DiIulio Jr. argues that tough criminal justice measures are needed to combat juvenile crime. Mike Males and Faye Docuyanan contend that this approach is ineffective and may even contribute to the problem. What are the main points made in support of each position? Which viewpoint presents its case most persuasively? Explain.

2. The Coalition for Juvenile Justice believes that some juveniles should be tried and sentenced as adults, but it contends that this action should be taken only as a last resort. What reasons does the coalition give for taking this position? Do you agree with the coalition? Why or why not?

3. From your reading of the viewpoints on curfew ordinances, do you think such laws unduly infringe on young people's freedoms? Or are the laws justified by their potential to save lives? Support your answer with examples from the viewpoints.

Organizations to Contact

The editors have compiled the following list of organizations concerned with the issues debated in this book. The descriptions are derived from materials provided by the organizations. All have publications or information available for interested readers. The list was compiled on the date of publication of the present volume; names, addresses, phone and fax numbers, and e-mail addresses may change. Be aware that many organizations take several weeks or longer to respond to inquiries, so allow as much time as possible.

ABA Juvenile Justice Center
740 15th St. NW
Washington, DC 20005
(202) 662-1515
fax: (202) 662-1501
internet: HN375@handsnet.org

An organization of the American Bar Association, the Juvenile Justice Center disseminates information on juvenile justice systems across the country. The center provides leadership to state and local practitioners, bar associations, judges, youth workers, correctional agency staff, and policymakers. Its publications include the book *Checklist for Use in Juvenile Delinquency Proceedings*, the report *America's Children at Risk*, and the quarterly *Criminal Justice Magazine*.

American Civil Liberties Union (ACLU)
132 W. 43rd St.
New York, NY 10036
(212) 944-9800
fax: (212) 869-9065

The ACLU is a national organization that works to defend Americans' civil rights as guaranteed by the U.S. Constitution. It opposes curfew laws for juveniles and others and seeks to protect the public-assembly rights of gang members or people associated with gangs. Among the ACLU's numerous publications are the book *In Defense of American Liberties: A History of the ACLU*, the handbook *The Rights of Prisoners: A Comprehensive Guide to the Legal Rights of Prisoners Under Current Law*, and the briefing paper "Crime and Civil Liberties."

American Correctional Association (ACA)
4380 Forbes Blvd.
Lanham, MD 20706
(301) 918-1800
fax: (301) 918-1900

The ACA is composed of correctional administrators, prison wardens, superintendents, and other corrections professionals who want to improve correctional standards. The ACA studies the causes of crime and juvenile delinquency and reports regularly on juvenile justice issues in its newsletter *On the Line*, which is published five times a year.

California Youth Authority Gang Violence Reduction Policy
2445 N. Mariondale Ave., Suite 202
Los Angeles, CA 90032-3516
(213) 227-4114
fax: (213) 227-5169

Operated by state parole agents, the project's goal is to mediate feuds among gangs in East Los Angeles. Its activities include developing job opportunities for former gang members, removing graffiti, and establishing parents groups. Staff members speak to organizations about prevention and other topics related to youth gangs. The project publishes a directory of organizations concerned with gangs as well as various pamphlets, including *Facts on Gangs* and *A Parent's Guide to Children's Problems*.

Center for the Study of Youth Policy
University of Pennsylvania School of Social Work
4200 Pine St., 2nd Fl.
Philadelphia, PA 19104-4090
(215) 898-2229
fax: (215) 573-2791

The center studies issues concerning juvenile justice and youth corrections. Although the center itself does not take positions regarding these issues, it publishes individuals' opinions in booklets, including *Home-Based Services for Serious and Violent Juvenile Offenders*, *Youth Violence: An Overview*, and *Mediation Involving Juveniles: Ethical Dilemmas and Policy Questions*.

Children of the Night
14530 Sylvan St.
Van Nuys, CA 91411
(818) 908-4474
crisis hotline: (800)-551-1300
fax: (818) 908-1468

Children of the Night provides protection and support for street children, usually runaways, who are involved in pornography or prostitution. The organization places children with counselors and in drug programs and independent living situations, and it conducts a semiannual training laboratory for persons who wish to work with street children. Children of the Night publishes a variety of brochures.

Committee for Children
2203 Airport Way S., Suite 500
Seattle, WA 98134-2027
(206) 343-1223
toll-free: (800)-634-4449
fax: (206) 343-1445

The Committee for Children is an international organization that develops classroom curricula and videos as well as teacher, parent, and community training programs for the prevention of child abuse and youth violence. *Second Step*, the committee's violence prevention curriculum, teaches children social skills and provides training for parents and teachers to practice and reinforce these skills with children. The committee publishes the newsletter *Prevention Update* three times a year and the video *What Do I Say Now? How to Help Protect Your Child from Sexual Abuse*.

Educational Fund to End Handgun Violence
100 Maryland Ave. NE, Suite 402
Washington, DC 20002
(202) 544-7214
fax: (202) 544-7213
e-mail: edfund@aol.com

The fund examines and helps educate the public about handgun violence in the United States and how such violence affects children in particular. The fund participates in the development of educational materials and programs to help persuade teenagers not to carry guns, and it examines the impact of handguns on public health. Its publications include the booklet *Kids and Guns: A National Disgrace* and the quarterly newsletters *Assault Weapon and Accessories in America* and *Firearms Litigation Reporter*.

Gang Violence Bridging Project
Edmund G. "Pat" Brown Institute of Public Affairs
California State University
5151 State University Dr.
Los Angeles, CA 90032-8261
(213) 343-3770
fax: (213) 343-3774

The project seeks to create communication among communities in the Los Angeles area. As an alternative to traditional suppressive measures such as incarceration, it advocates development of services and policies designed to prevent gang activity and to provide alternatives to gang membership. The project believes that the problem of gang violence must be addressed in the context of poverty, unemployment, and deteriorating schools and youth services. It publishes fact sheets on gang violence and related topics and a periodic newsletter, *PBI*.

The Heritage Foundation
214 Massachusetts Ave. NE
Washington, DC 20002
(202) 546-4400
fax: (202) 546-8328

The Heritage Foundation is a conservative public policy research institute. It advocates tougher sentences and the construction of more prisons as means to reduce crime. The foundation publishes the quarterly journal *Policy Review*, which occasionally contains articles addressing juvenile crime.

Milton S. Eisenhower Foundation
1660 L St. NW, Suite 200
Washington, DC 20036
(202) 429-0440
fax: (202) 452-0169

The foundation consists of individuals dedicated to reducing crime in inner-city neighborhoods through community programs. It believes that more federally funded programs such as Head Start and Job Corps would improve education and job opportunities for youths, thus reducing juvenile crime and violence. The foundation's publications include the report *Youth Investment and Community Reconstruction* and the book *The State of Families*.

National Association of Juvenile Correctional Agencies (NAJCA)
55 Albin Rd.
Bow, NH 03304-3703
(603) 224-9749

NAJCA promotes research and legislation that will improve the juvenile justice system. It opposes the death penalty for juveniles and the placement of juvenile offenders in adult prisons. NAJCA publishes the quarterly newsletter *NAJCA News* and the annual journal the *Proceedings*.

National Center on Institutions and Alternatives (NCIA)
635 Slaters Lane, Suite G-100
Alexandria, VA 22314
(703) 684-0373
fax: (703) 684-6037

The NCIA works to reduce the number of people institutionalized in prisons and mental hospitals. It favors the least restrictive forms of detention for juvenile offenders and opposes sentencing juveniles as adults and executing juvenile murderers. The NCIA publishes the books *The Real War on Crime* and *Search and Destroy: African-American Males in the Criminal Justice System*.

National Council of Juvenile and Family Court Judges
PO Box 8970
University of Nevada
Reno, NV 89557
(702) 784-6012
fax: (702) 784-6628

The council is composed of juvenile and family court judges and other juvenile justice professionals. It seeks to improve juvenile and family court standards and practices. Its publications include the monthly *Juvenile and Family Law Digest* and the quarterly *Juvenile and Family Court Journal*.

National Council on Crime and Delinquency (NCCD)
685 Market St., Suite 620
San Francisco, CA 94105
(415) 896-6223
fax: (415) 896-5109

The NCCD is composed of corrections specialists and others interested in the juvenile justice system and the prevention of crime and delinquency. It advocates community-based treatment programs rather than imprisonment for delinquent youths. It opposes placing minors in adult jails and executing those who commit capital offenses before the age of eighteen. The NCCD publishes the quarterlies *Crime and Delinquency* and *Journal of Research in Crime and Delinquency* as well as policy papers, including the "Juvenile Justice Policy Statement" and "Unlocking Juvenile Corrections: Evaluating the Massachusetts Department of Youth Services."

National Crime Prevention Council (NCPC)
1700 K St. NW, 2nd Fl.
Washington, DC 20006-3817
(202) 466-6272
fax: (202) 296-1356

The NCPC provides training and technical assistance to groups and individuals interested in crime prevention. It advocates job training and recreation programs as means to reduce youth crime and violence. The council, which sponsors the Take a Bite Out of Crime campaign, publishes the book *Preventing Violence: Program Ideas and Examples*, the booklet *How Communities Can Bring Up Youth Free from Fear and Violence*, and the newsletter *Catalyst*, which is published ten times a year.

National Criminal Justice Association (NCJA)
444 N. Capitol St. NW, Suite 618
Washington, DC 20001
(202) 347-4900
fax: (202) 508-3859

The NCJA is an association of state and local police chiefs, judges, attorneys, and other criminal justice officials that seeks to improve the administration of state criminal and juvenile justice programs. It publishes the monthly newsletter *Justice Bulletin*.

National School Safety Center (NSSC)
4165 Thousand Oaks Blvd., Suite 290
Westlake Village, CA 91362
(805) 373-9977
fax: (805) 373-9277

The NSSC is a research organization that studies school crime and violence, including hate crimes. The center believes that teacher training is an effective means of reducing these problems. Its publications include the book *Gangs in Schools: Breaking Up Is Hard to Do* and the *School Safety Update* newsletter, which is published nine times a year.

206

Office of Juvenile Justice and Delinquency Prevention (OJJDP)
633 Indiana Ave. NW
Washington, DC 20531
(202) 307-5911
fax: (202) 307-2093

As the primary federal agency charged with monitoring and improving the juvenile justice system, the OJJDP develops and funds programs on juvenile justice. Among its goals are the prevention and control of illegal drug use and serious crime by juveniles. Through its Juvenile Justice Clearinghouse, the OJJDP distributes fact sheets and reports such as *How Juveniles Get to Criminal Court*, *Gang Suppression and Intervention: Community Models*, and *Minorities and the Juvenile Justice System*.

Youth Crime Watch of America
9300 S. Dadeland Blvd., Suite 100
Miami, FL 33156
(305) 670-2409
fax: (305) 670-3805

Youth Crime Watch of America is dedicated to establishing Youth Crime Watch programs across the United States. It strives to give youths the tools and guidance necessary to actively reduce crime and drug use in their schools and communities. Its publications include *Talking to Youth About Crime Prevention*, the workbook *Community Based Youth Crime Watch Program Handbook*, and the motivational video *A Call for Young Heroes*.

Youth Policy Institute (YPI)
1333 Green Court St. NW
Washington, DC 20005
(202) 638-2144
fax: (202) 638-2325

The YPI monitors federal policies concerning youth and family in order to provide information on these policies to organizations and individuals. The institute believes that much of youth violence results from violence on television and in movies. It also believes that schools and local communities should try to solve the problem of youth violence. The YPI publishes the monthly magazines *American Family* and *Youth Policy*, the triannual journal *Future Choices*, and the biweekly *Youth Record*.

Bibliography of Books

Jay S. Albanese — *Dealing with Delinquency: The Future of Juvenile Justice.* Chicago: Nelson-Hall, 1993.

Ruth M. Alexander — *The Girl Problem: Female Sexual Delinquency in New York, 1900–1930.* Ithaca, NY: Cornell University Press, 1995.

Paul Almonte and Theresa Desmond — *Street Gangs.* New York: Crestwood House, 1994.

Simon Anderson et al. — *Cautionary Tales: Young People, Crime, and Policing in Edinburgh.* Brookfield, VT: Avebury, 1994.

Howard E. Barbaree, William L. Marshall, and Stephen M. Hudson, eds. — *The Juvenile Sex Offender.* New York: Guilford Press, 1993.

California Legislature, Task Force on School Violence — *Hearing on How Safe Are Our Children?* Sacramento, 1993.

California Legislature, Task Force on School Violence — *Hearing on Violence on Campuses.* Sacramento, 1993.

California Legislature, Committee on Education, Subcommittee on School Safety — *Stop the Violence! I Want to Learn.* Sacramento, 1994.

Annette Carrel — *It's the Law! A Young Person's Guide to Our Legal System.* Volcano, CA: Volcano Press, 1994.

Meda Chesney-Lind and Randall G. Shelden — *Girls, Delinquency, and Juvenile Justice.* New York: ACA Publications, 1992.

Yuet-wah Cheung — *Predicting Adolescent Deviant Behavior in Hong Kong: A Comparison of Media, Family, School, and Peer Variables.* Hong Kong: Hong Kong Institute of Asia-Pacific Studies, Chinese University of Hong Kong, 1993.

George Comstock — *Television and the American Child.* San Diego, CA: Academic Press, 1991.

Clifton Curry — *Juvenile Crime: Outlook for California.* Sacramento: Legislative Analyst's Office, 1995.

Shirley Dicks — *Young Blood: Juvenile Justice and the Death Penalty.* Amherst, NY: Prometheus Books, 1995.

Anthony N. Doob, Voula Marinos, and Kimberly N. Varma	*Youth Crime and the Youth Justice System in Canada: A Research Perspective*. Toronto: Centre of Criminology, University of Toronto, 1995.
Leonard D. Eron, Jacquelyn H. Gentry, and Peggy Schlegel, eds.	*Reason to Hope: A Psychosocial Perspective on Violence and Youth*. Washington, DC: American Psychological Association, 1994.
Brenda Geiger	*Family, Justice, and Delinquency*. Westport, CT: Greenwood Press, 1995.
Joan Gittens	*Poor Relations: The Children of the State in Illinois, 1818–1990*. Urbana: University of Illinois Press, 1994.
Arnold P. Goldstein	*Delinquents on Delinquency*. New York: ACA Publications, 1990.
John Hagan, ed.	*Delinquency and Disrepute in the Life Course*. Greenwich, CT: JAI Press, 1995.
Ann Hagell and Tim Newburn	*Young Offenders and the Media: Viewing Habits and Preferences* London: Policy Studies Institute, 1994.
Eugene E. Hebert	*Doing Something About Children at Risk*. Washington, DC: National Institute of Justice, 1993.
Kathleen M. Heide	*Why Kids Kill Parents: Child Abuse and Adolescent Homicide*. Thousand Oaks, CA: Sage Publications, 1995.
Paul C. Holinger et al.	*Suicide and Homicide Among Adolescents*. New York: Guilford Press, 1994.
James C. Howell et al., eds.	*Serious, Violent, and Chronic Juvenile Offenders: A Sourcebook*. Thousand Oaks, CA: Sage Publications, 1995.
James A. Inciardi, Ruth Horowitz, and Anne E. Pottieger	*Street Kids, Street Drugs, Street Crime: An Examination of Drug Use and Serious Delinquency in Miami*. Belmont, CA: Wadsworth, 1993.
Martín Sánchez Jankowski	*Islands in the Street: Gangs and American Urban Society*. Berkeley & Los Angeles: University of California Press, 1992.
Michael A. Jones and Barry Krisberg	*Images and Reality: Juvenile Crime, Youth Violence, and Public Policy*. San Francisco: National Council on Crime and Delinquency, 1994.
Josine Junger-Tas, Gert-Jan Terlouw, and Malcolm W. Klein, eds.	*Delinquent Behavior Among Young People in the Western World: First Results of the International Self-Report Delinquency Study*. New York: Kugler Publications, 1994.
Karen L. Kinnear	*Violent Children: A Research Handbook*. Santa Barbara, CA: ABC-CLIO, 1995.

209

Malcolm W. Klein   *The American Street Gang: Its Nature, Prevalence, and Control*. New York: Oxford University Press, 1995.

George W. Knox   *An Introduction to Gangs*. New York: ACA Publications, 1994.

Kimberly Kempf Leonard, ed.   *Minorities in Juvenile Justice*. Thousand Oaks, CA: Sage Publications, 1995.

William J. Mackey, Janet Fredericks, and Marcel A. Fredericks   *Urbanism as Delinquency: Compromising the Agenda for Social Change*. Lanham, MD: University Press of America, 1993.

Marc Mauer   *Young Black Men and the Criminal Justice System: A Growing National Problem*. Washington, DC: Sentencing Project, 1990.

Jerome G. Miller   *Hobbling a Generation: Young African-American Males in Washington, D.C.'s Criminal Justice System*. Washington, DC: National Center on Institutions and Alternatives, 1992.

Paul Mones   *When a Child Kills: Abused Children Who Kill Their Parents*. New York: Pocket Books, 1991.

David Musick   *An Introduction to the Sociology of Juvenile Delinquency*. Albany: State University of New York Press, 1995.

National Issues   *Kids Who Commit Crimes: What Should Be Done About Juvenile Violence?* Dubuque, IA: Kendall/Hunt, 1994.

Mike Rose   *Possible Lives: The Promise of Public Education in America*. Boston: Houghton Mifflin, 1995.

Gail D. Ryan and Sandra Lane, eds.   *Juvenile Sexual Offending: Causes, Consequences, and Correction*. Lexington, MA: Lexington Books, 1991.

Robert J. Sampson and John H. Laub   *Crime in the Making: Pathways and Turning Points Through Life*. Cambridge, MA: Harvard University Press, 1993.

William B. Sanders   *Gangbangs and Drive-Bys: Grounded Culture and Juvenile Gang Violence*. New York: Aldine de Gruyter, 1994.

Joseph F. Sheley and James D. Wright   *In the Line of Fire: Youths, Guns, and Violence in Urban America*. New York: Aldine de Gruyter, 1995.

Michelle Slatella and Joshua Quittner   *Masters of Deception: The Gang That Rules Cyberspace*. New York: HarperCollins, 1995.

Irving A. Spergel   *The Youth Gang Problem: A Community Approach*. New York: Oxford University Press, 1995.

Martha B. Straus   *Violence in the Lives of Adolescents*. New York: Norton, 1994.

Dorothy L. Taylor   *The Positive Influence of Bonding in Female-Headed African American Families*. New York: Garland, 1993.

Tony Waters and Lawrence E. Cohen   *Laotians in the Criminal Justice System*. Berkeley: California Policy Seminar, 1993.

Rob White and Christine Alder, eds.   *The Police and Young People in Australia*. Cambridge University Press, 1994.

Kevin N. Wright and Karen E. Wright   *Family Life, Delinquency, and Crime: A Policymaker's Guide*. Washington, DC: Office of Juvenile Justice and Delinquency Prevention, 1994.

Index

215

curfew laws, 189-92, 194-96
  on gangs, 134-35, 194
  on juveniles being tried as adults,
    175-79, 181
  STOP law, 166
  three-strikes laws, 163, 165
Lewis, Dorothy Otnow, 79, 81, 185
Lichter, S. Robert, 59
Little Rock, Ark.
  crime rate in, 158
  curfew in, 194
Loeber, Rolf, 70, 71
Los Angeles, Calif.
  crime rate in, 158
  curfew in, 194
  gangs in, 121, 131, 133-35, 169-70
  guns in schools in, 18
  riots in, 42, 121, 131
  teenage murders in, 169-70
Loury, Glenn, 115

Maginnis, Robert L., 62
Males, Mike, 167
marriage
  prevents crime, 64-65, 89
  troubles affect children, 70, 71
  see also families
Married . . . with Children (TV series),
  61
Masterpiece Theatre (TV series), 57, 58
Matsueda, Ross L., 68
McBride, Wes, 150, 152
McDowell, David, 185
McLanahan, Sara, 71, 73
media
  blame juveniles for crime, 42-44,
    181
  and discrimination, 123, 125-27
  publicizing crime, 25, 38
  reform of, 61
  violence in, 53, 63, 76, 80-81
Mednick, Birgitte R., 71
Meet the Press (TV series), 42
men
  biological indicators of criminality
    in, 77
  crime statistics on, 79, 110-11,
    163-64, 171
  fathers' effect on children, 64, 70
  homicide by, 91
  and inner-city culture, 104-105
  marriage civilizes, 64-65
  and testosterone, 79
Metsger, Linda, 185
Miami, Fla., curfew in, 194
Michigan
  juvenile justice system in, 183
  see also Detroit

Mighty Morphin' Power Rangers (TV
  series), 57
Mikawa, James K., 70
Milwaukee, Wis., curfew in, 158
minorities
  curfews discriminate against, 195-96
  and gangs, 38, 110, 131, 137, 172
  imprisonment of, 172
  and poverty, 168, 172
  see also blacks; Hispanics
Minow, Newton, 58
Mitchell, David B., 22
Moles, Oliver, 36
Moore, Mark H., 47
Morash, Merry, 73
Mothers Against Gangs in Chicago,
  153
Motion Picture Association of
  America, 61
movie violence, 60, 61
murder
  by blacks, 91-92, 94, 109, 170
  of children, 18, 19, 76, 94
  of exchange students, 42
  in Florida, 42, 43
  and gangs, 131, 133-35, 194
  by Hispanics, 170
  by juveniles, 19-20, 26, 63, 64, 76,
    80, 169, 178
    increase in, 18, 47, 63, 91, 109
  predominates among acquaintances,
    92
  reduction in, 158
  statistics on, 25, 64, 91-94, 109-10,
    168
  of tourists, 42
Murder She Wrote (TV series), 58
Murray, Cecil, 125
Murray, David W., 65
Muslims, 128-29
Myles, Dee, 69
Mystery! (TV series), 58

Nassef, Ahmed, 120
Nate II, 120
National Advisory Committee on
  Criminal Justice Standards and
  Goals, 188
National Association of Broadcasters,
  61
National Center for Juvenile Justice,
  47, 76
National Commission on Crime
  Control and Prevention, 114
National Council on Crime and
  Delinquency (NCCD), 188
National Incidence Studies on
  Missing, Abducted, Runaway, and

217

Wartik, Nancy, 75
Washington, Adrienne T., 197
Washington, D.C.
  curfew in, 194
  police in, 160
Washington state, three-strikes law
  in, 165
Wattenberg, Ben, 162
Wattenberg's Law, 162
Webster-Stratton, Carolyn, 69
Weinstein, Deena, 66
Weisenburger, William, 38
Wells, L. Edward, 68, 71, 72
West, Cornel, 115
"whirlpooling," 46
White, Helene Raskin, 70
whites
  discrimination by, 121-29
  promote drugs, 121, 123
  social system of, 121, 127-28, 196-98
Wildmon, Donald, 61
Will, George, 43

Wilson, James Q., 63, 111, 170, 186
Wisconsin
  curfew in, 158
  gangs in, 135
  juvenile justice system in, 168
Wolfgang, Marvin, 48
women
  attitudes toward, 48
  biological indicators of criminality
    in, 78
  as gang members, 152
  and inner-city culture, 99, 105-106
  as responsible for male violence, 69
  in single-parent families, 64, 68-69,
    71-72, 86, 97, 99-100, 146
Wright, Karen E., 67
Wright, Kevin N., 67

Young Riders, The (TV series), 59

Zeeb, Linda, 69
Zuckerman, Mortimer B., 52